## Table of Measures

| | |
|---|---|
| Pinch or dash . . . | less than ⅛ teaspoon |
| 1 tablespoon . . | 3 teaspoons |
| 2 tablespoons . . | 1 fluid ounce |
| ¼ cup . . . . | 4 tablespoons |
| ⅓ cup . . . . | 5 tablespoons plus 1 teaspoon |
| ½ cup . . . . | 8 tablespoons |
| 1 cup . . . . | 16 tablespoons |
| 1 cup . . . . | 8 fluid ounces |
| 1 pint . . . . | 2 cups |
| 1 quart . . . . | 4 cups |
| 4 quarts . . . . | 1 gallon |
| ¼ pound . . . | 4 ounces |
| 1 pound . . . . | 16 ounces |

## Baking Time Table

| | Temperature | Time |
|---|---|---|
| **CAKES:** | | |
| Cupcakes . . . . . | 350°F.-375°F. | 20 to 30 min. |
| Foam- or sponge-type . | 350°F.-375°F. | 30 to 60 min. |
| Fruit cakes . . . . . | 275°F.-300°F. | 2 hrs. or more |
| Jelly roll . . . . . | 400°F. | 12 to 15 min. |
| Pound cakes . . . . | 300°F.-325°F. | 1 to 1½ hrs. |
| Rectangular cakes . . | 350°F.-375°F. | 35 to 45 min. |
| Round or square layers | 350°F.-375°F. | 25 to 40 min. |
| **COOKIES:** | | |
| Bar . . . . . . . | 350°F.-375°F. | 20 to 35 min. |
| Drop . . . . . . . | 350°F.-375°F. | 10 to 15 min. |
| Shaped or rolled . . . | 375°F.-400°F. | 8 to 12 min. |
| **PIES:** | | |
| Custard . . . . . . | 400°F.-425°F. | 30 to 45 min. |
| Fruit . . . . . . . | 425°F. | 45 to 60 min. |
| Meringue . . . . . | 425°F. | 5 to 8 min. |
| Pie and tart shells . . | 450°F. | 12 to 15 min. |
| **QUICK BREADS:** | | |
| Biscuits . . . . . . | 450°F. | 10 to 15 min. |
| Coffee cakes, muffins . | 375°F.-425°F. | 25 to 35 min. |
| Fruit and nut loaves . | 350°F. | 55 to 75 min. |
| **YEAST BREADS:** | | |
| Dinner rolls . . . . | 375°F.-400°F. | 15 to 20 min. |
| Loaves . . . . . . | 375°F.-400°F. | 45 to 55 min. |
| Sweet rolls, coffee cake | 350°F.-400°F. | 20 to 35 min. |

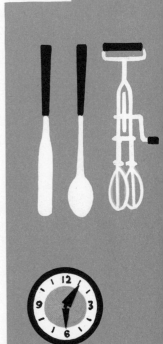

# All About Home Baking

## BY GENERAL FOODS KITCHENS

*Drawings by* MARY RONIN
*Cover photographs by* NORMAN KARLSON

## RANDOM HOUSE

# Contents

*Black and Gold Marble Cake (p. 38) with Fluffy Chocolate Butter Frosting (p. 60) makes a delightful party dessert or the feature attraction for afternoon tea.*

## SECTION 1

GENERAL FOODS
KITCHENS

# Baking Facts and Figures

### A WORD OR TWO ABOUT THIS AND THAT

Baking is an art — you are the artist. The materials of this art are such common things as eggs, flour, and sugar. The brush is a mixing spoon and the canvas is, of course, your dinner table.

Time was when apprenticeship, experience, and trial and error were the only means of mastering this art. Because we now have such things as tested recipes and standard measuring equipment, even the beginner just learning her way around the kitchen can be reasonably sure her very first cake will be high, light, tender, and delicious, if she follows directions.

After choosing a recipe that sounds particularly good, read it through from first word to last. Have a nodding acquaintance with the recipe before you even get out a mixing bowl. See that you have all the necessary ingredients — halfway through is an unfortunate time to find you have only 2 eggs for the 3-egg cake you're making. Better still, get out all the ingredients you'll need. Cookies, cakes, and breads are all easier to mix and better, too, when ingredients are at room temperature (unless otherwise directed).

1

And while you're checking, make sure you have the right size pan for baking. If not, there may be one you can substitute. (See page 21 for pan sizes and substitutions.)

If unfamiliar words or procedures are used in a recipe, investigate first. Mistakes made through misunderstood words make funny stories (such as the novice who "creamed" the shortening by adding a goodly splash of heavy cream) but very poor cakes, pies, and cookies.

In perfecting the recipes in this book, we have carefully chosen, balanced, and combined each and every ingredient. If you alter amounts of ingredients, especially such key ingredients as flour, sugar, shortening, and liquid, you are flirting with failure. If, for example, you've added the one-half cup milk a cake recipe calls for and you feel the batter is too stiff, don't add another tablespoon or two to make it more to your liking. The batter is supposed to be that stiff, ½ cup milk is all that is required.

Substituting can be dangerous, too. For instance, a recipe calling for dried apricots means just that. Don't substitute canned or fresh apricots — either get some dried apricots or use another recipe.

Frequently one seasoning or flavoring can be substituted for another. If a recipe calls for grated lemon rind, grated orange rind will change only the flavor. If a cake is flavored with cinnamon and you like nutmeg, chances are that you can make the substitution. Substitute with caution since flavorings and seasonings are not always the same strength.

Doubling a recipe usually means trouble, especially in baking. It may take an additional minute or two, but you'll save money and time in the long run if you make up the exact recipe as many times as needed.

The first three sections of this book are concerned with the three vital steps in baking: measuring, mixing, and baking. They are full of information and baking tips gathered by us at General Foods Kitchens through years of testing and tasting experience. Even an old hand with the mixing bowl may pick up a fact or two that will be of value.

## MEASURING UP TO THE RECIPE

At least half the secret of baking a good cake, cooky, or loaf of bread is the measuring. When developing recipes for this book we used only *standard measuring cups and spoons,* and all of our measurements were *level.* In order to obtain our same good results from these recipes, you must do likewise. If you don't have some standard measuring equipment among your possessions, invest in some, it's worth the cost. Here's what you should have.

*For dry ingredients:* One 1-cup graduated measuring cup with the 1-cup line at the rim and/or a nest of 4 measuring cups including a ¼-cup, ⅓-cup, ½-cup, and a 1-cup measurer.

*For liquid ingredients:* A measuring cup with the 1-cup line below the rim of the cup is best. This allows you to measure liquids accurately without spilling. This type of measuring cup is frequently found in glass and is available not only in the 1-cup size, but in 2-cup and 1-quart sizes as well. The 1 cup is essential; all are handy.

*Measuring spoons:* These usually come in sets hooked together by a ring. Each set includes a ¼ teaspoon, ½ teaspoon, 1 teaspoon, and a 1 tablespoon measurer.

*Flour:* Flour has a tendency to pack and the finer the flour the more it packs. The only way to be sure 1 cup of flour is actually 1 cup is to sift it first, then measure. Sift it onto a square of paper, a paper plate, or into a bowl. Spoon this flour into a measuring cup, heaping it up slightly. Then level off excess with a straight edge, not the flat surface, of a spatula or knife. Never shake a cup to level it off. And never sift flour directly into a measuring cup. This gives you *less* than a standard measuring cup of flour.

*Granulated and confectioners' sugar:* If sugar is at all lumpy (confectioners' sugar often is) sift it first. Then spoon it into a cup, heaping it slightly. Level off the excess with the edge of a spatula or knife.

*Brown sugar:* There is only one way to measure brown sugar accurately — *pack it firmly* into a cup or spoon. It should be packed so well that, when turned out of a cup, it will hold its shape. If brown sugar is at all lumpy, sift it through a coarse sieve before measuring.

*Baking powder, salt, etc.:* When measuring ingredients such as baking powder, soda, salt, and spices, dip a measuring spoon (dry, of course) of the correct size into the ingredient and lift it out slightly heaped. Level it off with the edge of a spatula or knife. Some ingredient containers, such as Calumet Baking Powder, come equipped with a paper covering that can be cut and used as a "leveler."

Baking powder should always be stored tightly covered since it has a tendency to absorb moisture and thus lose leavening power. It is false economy to keep baking powder on the shelf for more than a year. If it fails to act with the proper degree of potency, the expense of the other ingredients that are wasted far exceeds the cost of a fresh can of baking powder.

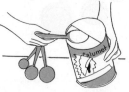

*Shortening, butter, margarine:* Spoon shortening from a can or package and pack firmly into a graduated measuring cup so that no air bubbles are left along the bottom or sides. Level it off even with the rim of the cup using the edge of a spatula or knife. When removing the shortening from a cup, use a rubber scraper or something equally pliable so that no shortening is left clinging to the sides of the cup.

Butter or margarine can be measured in the same way. Or if butter or margarine (and sometimes lard) is packaged in a 1-pound print, remember that each ¼ pound stick equals ½ cup. Frequently the wrappers on these sticks indicate where to cut for 1-tablespoon measures, too.

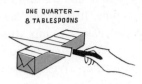

ONE QUARTER — 8 TABLESPOONS

If a recipe calls for melted fat, we find it makes no difference whether it is measured before or after melting. To measure melted fat or salad oil, pour it into a measuring spoon or cup to the level of the rim or measuring line.

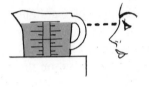

*Liquids:* Use a standard measuring cup with the rim above the 1-cup marker. Set the cup on a level surface. Fill the cup to the desired mark, checking it at eye level. (Yes, do a deep knee bend, if necessary.)

To measure thick liquids such as molasses and syrup, pour the liquid into the measuring cup or spoon. Never dip into the liquid since it will coat the outside of the spoon, giving you an over-measure. Syrup heaps slightly, so level it off with a spatula or knife.

SYRUP

*Eggs:* Because hens are individualists, eggs vary in size. They are usually available in both medium and large sizes. When a recipe calls for 3 eggs, chances are 3 medium-sized eggs are required. A good rule of thumb for substitution is to remember 2 large eggs equal 3 small ones. If a recipe gives a cup measurement for eggs it is wise to use it rather than number. Few recipes call for half an egg, but should you need one the only way to divide an egg is to beat it thoroughly, measure, then divide.

## BAKING'S MAGIC WAND

The mixing spoon is baking's magic wand, for we think there is a kind of magic in taking such everyday ingredients as flour, eggs, sugar, and milk and transforming them into high, light, and lovely cakes or tender muffins. It is during the mixing that ingredients are blended and a change takes place. So mix with care and keep in mind the following suggestions.

*Equipment:* The kind of mixing spoon you use is strictly a personal preference. We like wooden ones simply because they are more comfortable. Your mixing bowl should be large enough to allow the batter to be beaten vigorously without an overflow. For good all-purpose mixing bowls, choose pottery, glass, or stainless steel. Since egg whites do not whip properly in some kinds of soft plastic bowls, it's best to avoid such bowls for mixing sponge-type cakes and meringue mixtures. A damp cloth placed under the bowl prevents slipping and sliding during mixing.

An electric mixer, standard-size or portable, makes pure pleasure out of the beating chore once associated with baking. There are some differences in the two kinds of mixers since the portable has only three speeds while standard mixers may have 10 or more. The low or first speed on the portable can be equated with the low or first three or four speeds on standard mixers. The second speed on the portable equals the medium or fourth and fifth through the seventh or eighth speeds on standard mixers. The third or high speed on portables will do the whipping and fast beating that the higher speeds of standard mixers do. Electric mixers are not in any way essential; one willing arm will take their place any day.

One of the handiest items, not only for baking but for any kind of cooking, is a rubber scraper. It gets out the last bit of shortening from the measuring cup, cleans the sides of the bowl during mixing and wipes it clean as a whistle when you're pouring the batter into pans. (The small fry may not appreciate this last usage.)

It is hard to say whether a sifter should be classed under measuring or mixing equipment since it is necessary for both. In any case have a large sturdy one. In lieu of a sifter, use a large, fine wire sieve.

Metal cooling racks are very, very handy. They allow cookies, cakes, breads — all kinds of baked products to cool evenly with a free circulation of air. Have two racks, if possible.

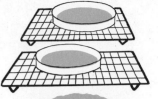

There are other utensils that are very useful for mixing, such as slotted spoons and wire whisks, but these are added helps, not essentials.

## INGREDIENTS AND METHODS

There are certain essential ingredients or types of ingredients used in all kinds of baking, and there are recommended methods of mixing these ingredients. But before you even begin mixing, always prepare your pans, then turn on the oven so it can pre-heat. Chop nuts and fruits, soak raisins, and do other such preparatory work, too, before the mixing begins.

*Shortening:* Butter, margarine, emulsifier-type shortening, lard, and salad oil can be and are all used in baking. But they are not always interchangeable. Butter and margarine usually contain some salt and are only about 80% fat. The other 20% consists of liquid and milk solids. Butter and margarine can be used interchangeably with usually only some slight difference in flavor.

Emulsified (or hydrogenated) shortenings, made from all vegetable fat or part vegetable and part animal fat, are creamy white (or yellow) in color, light, workable, and wonderfully easy to blend with other ingredients. Since these shortenings and lard contain little or no salt and are almost 100% fat, they can be used interchangeably in recipes. Here again the flavors differ. Emulsifier-type shortenings are very bland, having almost no flavor or aroma, while lard has a more or less distinct flavor.

Salad oil can be used in most recipes calling for melted shortening, but it's best to use it only when specified.

Most solid fats, butter, margarine, and emulsified shortenings can be used, with some adjustments, interchangeably. These adjustments apply mostly to cake recipes. Our general rule is when using butter or margarine in a recipe calling for shortening, decrease the liquid by 1 tablespoon for every ¼ to ⅓ cup of fat used in the recipe. The opposite is true when using shortening in a recipe calling for either butter or margarine.

You'll find, with one or two exceptions, the cake recipes in this book call for emulsified shortening. If any liquid adjustment is needed when using butter or margarine, we have made a note to that effect.

The standard methods of combining fats with other ingredients are:

*Cream together:* This is the method used for most standard shortening-type cakes and some cookies, and frostings. Creaming simply means working or beating the shortening with a spoon or a mixer until it is soft and "creamy." At this point sugar is beaten into the shortening, or "creamed" with the shortening. Both of these steps have been eliminated in mix-easy method cakes (see page 19).

*Cut in:* Shortening is cut into a flour mixture for biscuits, pastry, and in some cooky and muffin recipes. With two knives, or a pastry blender, use a cutting motion to work the shortening into the flour mixture.

*Melted:* Melted shortening and salad oil are usually added to dry ingredients along with liquid ingredients. Muffins, griddlecakes, and yeast breads usually call for melted shortening.

*Eggs:* Eggs are added in many ways — whole or separated, beaten or unbeaten, singly or all together. The method varies with the recipe.

*Whole eggs:* If added unbeaten, eggs should be beaten into the batter thoroughly, one at a time. If they are beaten before they are added eggs need only to be stirred or folded in.

*Egg whites:* When air is beaten into egg whites with a wire whisk, a rotary beater, or electric mixer the egg whites expand and become fluffy and stiff — thus the descriptive term "stiffly beaten." Because of the added air they act as leavening. In sponge- or foam-type cakes they are sometimes the *only* leavening. Egg whites beaten to the soft peak stage form rounded glossy peaks when the beater is lifted. If you continue beating, these peaks become stiffer, more pointed, but should retain their glossiness. Never beat egg whites so long that they lose this glossiness;

overbeaten egg whites become dry and begin to lose volume. Meringue, used as a pie topping and in some cakes and cookies, is made by adding sugar gradually, a tablespoon or two at a time, as egg whites are beaten. The sugar tends to stabilize beaten egg whites.

Stiffly beaten egg whites are almost always "folded" into a batter or other ingredients. To fold, pile all the egg whites on top of the batter at once. Then with a wire whisk, rubber scraper, or large spoon, cut down through the mixture, across the bottom, and lift some of the mixture up and over the egg whites. Continue this folding motion until the beaten egg whites are blended. Never beat or stir in whipped egg whites unless the recipe tells you to. This same folding method is used for adding thickly beaten eggs and egg yolks and whipped cream, too.

*Egg yolks:* These are added to many kinds and types of baked products, beaten or not as the recipe directs. If egg yolks are beaten for any length of time they begin to thicken and gradually lose color, becoming a rather pale lemon-yellow. As with egg whites, incorporated air causes the change in color and texture.

*Flour:* There are many kinds and types of flour, each with a more or less specific use. They vary because of the wheat from which they are made, when and where this wheat is grown, and the milling process. Cake flour, such as Swans Down Cake Flour, is milled from "soft" winter wheat into the finest, most delicate of flours. It is ideal to use for all kinds of tender textured cakes and some elegant quick breads and cookies.

All-purpose flour is exactly what its name implies. It can be used for all kinds of baking, but not with equally good results. All-purpose flour cakes are usually sturdier with a slightly coarser texture and crumb.

A self-rising flour has the leavening and the salt already added. When using it for cakes, biscuits, or muffins omit both the leavening and the salt called for in the recipe.

In most recipes the flour is mixed with the leavening and salt. In standard shortening-type cakes the flour is added to the creamed shortening-sugar mixture alternately with the liquid. Begin and end with flour

9

additions. Add about a quarter of the flour at a time and about a third of the liquid at a time. Beat the batter after each addition just until all the flour (or liquid) disappears.

In pastry and in some quick breads the shortening is cut into the flour mixture. In other quick breads and in most yeast breads the liquid ingredients are mixed with the flour mixture.

*Leavening:* Baking powder, such as Calumet, is the most common leavening. It is a combination of baking soda and dry acid ingredients. When baking powder is mixed with a liquid, the baking soda and acid react, releasing a gas which forms small even bubbles throughout the batter or dough. When the batter is baked these gas bubbles expand, causing the batter to rise and become light.

Calumet Baking Powder is double-acting, only part of the gas is released when it's mixed with a liquid. The additional gas is released only in the presence of heat, after the product is in the oven. This double-acting characteristic makes the baking powder more reliable and assures well-leavened cakes, biscuits, and muffins.

Buttermilk, molasses, some fruit juices, brown sugar, and chocolate are all acid ingredients. When used in recipes these acids are neutralized by baking soda. The gas produced by this neutralizing action acts as leavening. In some recipes both soda and baking powder are used because the gas produced by the soda-acid reaction is insufficient to leaven the product properly. The baking powder is added to increase the leavening.

*Liquids:* Milk, either sweet or buttermilk, is the liquid used most frequently in baking — water runs a close second. However, fruit juice, cream, and other liquids are often used for distinctive flavor and texture.

*Chocolate:* Since chocolate burns very easily, it should never be melted over direct heat. Place the chocolate (sweet or unsweetened) in a pan or bowl over hot, not boiling, water and stir occasionally until melted. Cool melted chocolate slightly before adding it to batter.

## BAKING AT HIGH ALTITUDES

When you live at altitudes of 3000 feet or over, baking, especially cake baking, presents problems. (Cookies, pastries, and breads present few problems other than adjusting baking temperatures upward by 10°F. to 15°F. when necessary.) We have gathered together the following information that will help you solve some of these problems, but maybe not all of them because individual recipes differ greatly.

*Shortening-type cakes:* Usually a decrease in sugar or leavening or both, and an increase in liquid are needed. We use the following table as a guide for these adjustments. Experiment with your own recipes to find the best adjustment for each recipe.

| Adjustment | 3000 ft. | 5000 ft. | 7000 ft. |
|---|---|---|---|
| *Baking Powder* for each teaspoon, decrease | ⅛ tsp. | ⅛ to ¼ tsp. | ¼ tsp. |
| *Sugar* for each cup, decrease | 1 tbsp. | 1 to 2 tbsp. | 2 to 3 tbsp. |
| *Liquid* for each cup, add | 1 to 2 tbsp. | 2 to 4 tbsp. | 3 to 4 tbsp. |

In addition to the above adjustments, very rich cakes may need a reduction in shortening by about 1 or 2 tablespoons. Cakes made with baking soda may need slightly less of this leavening. And a 10°F. to 15°F. increase in baking temperature may give better results for cupcakes and layer cakes.

*Sponge- or foam-type cakes:* Since air beaten into eggs is the leavening in these cakes, reduce it by decreasing the beating time. Over-beaten eggs at high altitudes cause dry cakes. At very high altitudes, you may have to use more eggs, but they should still be slightly underbeaten. The baking temperature for these cakes should be increased by 10°F. to 15°F. at 5000 ft. and at every 5000 ft. increase in altitude.

## THE HEAT TREATMENT

The last important step of baking takes place in the oven. In the heat of the oven baked products assume their finished color, taste, and texture. Sometimes only 5 or 10 minutes baking is needed for quick browning, at other times an hour or more is needed for thorough baking. Temperatures vary, too, from a low 300°F. to a high 500°F. But no matter what you are baking, how long, or at what temperature, the heat and time must be closely controlled.

What you are baking governs just how hot and how long. Follow recipe baking directions exactly, considering each cake and every batch of muffins individually. However, some generalizations can be made as to baking time and temperature. Should you have occasion to use a recipe without specific baking instructions, check the chart on the back inside cover of this book.

*Pans:* The size, shape, and the material from which a pan is made also affect baking. Our recipes, most recipes in fact, suggest the ideal pan size in which to bake. If you don't have the exact pan size called for, you'll find a chart on page 21 listing possible pan substitutions.

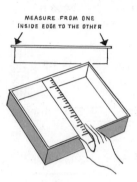

MEASURE FROM ONE INSIDE EDGE TO THE OTHER

Most baking pans you buy today are standardized, and manufacturers have stamped or marked the size on each pan. Look for these markings when buying pans. If your pans are collectors' items and assorted hand-me-down minus any markings — measure, then mark them yourself. Always measure from one top inside edge to the opposite inside edge.

We find that shiny baking pans are best for most baking, the shinier the better. Keep pans in good condition by cleaning them with steel-wool soap pads. Loaf pans, used for bread baking, and pie pans are exceptions to this rule. You'll get a richer, more golden brown crust on both pies and breads if these pans have a dull finish.

If you use oven-proof glass pans and find baked products brown too quickly or burn, try reducing the oven temperature by 25°F. We always reduce the temperature when baking cakes in glass pans.

*To grease or not to grease:* *Never* grease or treat in any way the pans in which sponge- or foam-type cakes are baked. The one exception to this rule is the jelly or cake roll pan. These pans should always be lined with greased paper.

All shortening-type cakes are baked in pans that have either been greased, greased and floured, or lined with paper. As a general rule the recipe states how the pan is to be treated. For most cakes the results are better, higher cakes with more level tops, if the sides of pans are not greased. Ungreased sides give cakes something to "climb on" during baking and present no problem when removing the cake since once around with a spatula loosens the cake. Whether you grease and flour or use a paper liner is up to you and your recipe. We find the paper-liner method better and easier. The paper does not have to reach the pan's edge or even fit the bottom exactly. An irregularly shaped piece of waxed paper, paper napkin or toweling, or brown paper placed in the center of the pan works just as well as a piece of paper cut carefully to fit the pan. In fact, we find it's better, for if the paper extends up the sides of the pan at all, it usually causes the bottom of the cake to be slightly misshapen.

If you do not line pans with paper, spread a *thin* layer of grease (emulsified shortening or salad oil is best for this) over the bottom.

To flour a greased pan, shake a spoonful of flour around in the pan until it is evenly coated. Remove excess by gently tapping the inverted pan.

Fluted paper cups or cupcake liners set in muffin pans are by far the best thing to use when baking cupcakes. A large supply of these paper liners costs very little, and they eliminate sticking and assure well rounded, nicely shaped cupcakes. If you don't use these cupcake liners, grease and flour only the bottoms of the muffin pans.

Cookies need various pan treatments depending largely upon the recipe. Rich cookies can be baked on ungreased sheets. Use greased pans for less rich cookies. Bar-type cookies should be baked in greased pans. Pastry need never be baked in a greased pan, it's rich enough. Most quick and yeast breads are baked in greased pans.

When pouring batter into a pan, spread it smoothly and well into all corners. Divide it evenly if you are using more than one pan. Cut through sponge-type cake batters in the pan to release large air bubbles that may have formed.

***Baking time and temperature:*** Always pre-heat your oven. Give it a chance to reach and maintain a steady temperature by turning it on while you prepare ingredients for mixing. This allows plenty of time. When you turn on the oven, check the racks to see that they are at or near the middle where the heat is most likely to be even.

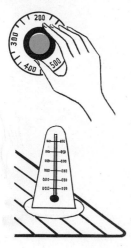

Some women can, with their hand, estimate an oven's temperature to within a few degrees. Some people have perfect pitch, too. Both are rare exceptions. You'll find a thermostat or an oven thermometer much more accurate. Most ovens now-a-days come equipped with a thermostatic control device that is a fairly accurate temperature regulator. If you consistently have trouble with products being either over or underbaked at the end of the recommended time, have your oven checked. It may be 25 or so degrees off. Because thermostats cannot be fully trusted, it is a good idea to equip yourself with an oven thermometer. And buy a good one, it's worth it.

When placing cakes, pies, or breads in the oven, be sure the pans are at or near the middle of the oven where the heat is most even. Leave space between each pan so the heat may circulate freely. And keep pans away from the oven walls for the same reason. If, in order not to crowd the pans, you must place them on different racks, stagger them so one is not directly over another.

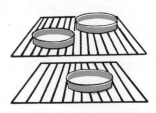

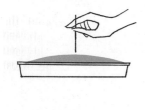

If the oven temperature is correct and the pan size is too, then the time needed for baking should be within the time range suggested in the recipe. Always test cakes at the minimum time given since ovens frequently vary 15°F. to 25°F. Here are two tests commonly used for cakes: open the oven door just enough to insert a cake tester or toothpick into the center of the cake. If the cake is done the tester will come out clean. Or, touch the cake lightly with a finger. If the cake springs back leaving no imprint, then the cake is done. If either test shows the cake is not done, bake it a few minutes longer, then test again.

Whatever you do, don't open the oven door before the minimum baking time has elapsed and never shift the pans around during baking — both are sure to cause failure.

## POST BAKING CARE

With some baked products, such as biscuits, yeast rolls, and muffins, the only care needed is quick eating — the faster the better. But loaves of yeast and nut or fruit bread should be removed from the pan and cooled on a rack before cutting. Nut and fruit breads have a better flavor and cut more easily if wrapped and stored for a day.

*Cooling pies and cookies:* Serve pies warm or cool, as you wish. Custard, cream, and meringue pies have a better consistency if cooled at least until they are lukewarm. Keep all cream- and custard-type pies in the refrigerator if storing for any length of time.

Cooky temperatures, too, are a matter of preference — some like 'em hot, some like 'em cold. In any case, dropped, shaped, and rolled cookies should be removed from baking sheets immediately (unless otherwise directed), then cooled on racks. Cool bar-type cookies in the pan, then cut. Store them in the pan tightly covered with aluminum foil or waxed paper.

Store crisp cookies and soft or moist cookies separately, never together, since crisp cookies quickly absorb moisture from soft ones. Empty coffee or shortening cans make fine cooky "jars."

*Cool cakes:* With only a few exceptions, all cakes should be thoroughly cooled before cutting or frosting. For proper cooling, air should circulate freely around all sides of the cake. Cakes placed on metal racks designed especially for this purpose cool quickly and evenly.

*Shortening-type cakes:* When a shortening-type cake is removed from the oven, place the pan right side up on a rack and let it stand for 10 to 15 minutes. Large rich cakes take the longest. Run a spatula or dull knife around the edge of the cake. Place a rack over the cake and invert both cake and rack, then lift the pan. If you've used paper to line the pan it will probably stick to the cake — peel it off. Then cover the cake with a second

rack and invert again so the cake cools thoroughly right side up. Although fruit cakes are shortening-type cakes, they may split wide open if taken from the pans while hot. We cool them in the pans until they are lukewarm, then remove and finish cooling them on racks.

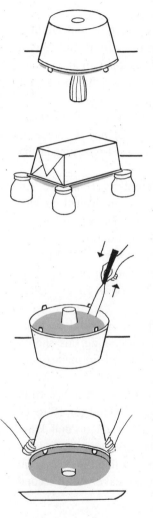

*Sponge- or foam-type cakes:* Because angel food, sponge, and chiffon cakes have an extremely fragile structure they must "hang" upside down while cooling. To do this, immediately upon taking one of these cakes from the oven turn it upside down, and let it cool for about 2 hours. If fully baked it will not fall out since the pan has not been greased or treated in any way. Tube pans, frequently used for sponge and angel food cakes, have a tube (hence the name) through the center which extends above the rim of the pan. The inverted cake may rest on this to allow free circulation of air. Or sometimes the pans have side "ears" upon which they may rest. If the tube pan has neither an extended center tube nor "ears," rest the tube over a narrow-necked bottle or inverted funnel. If sponge-type cakes are baked in layers, squares, or loaf pans, rest the edges of inverted pans on glass baking cups or anything else that will hold the cake away from the table surface and allow free circulation of air.

When the cake has cooled (usually about 2 hours) turn it right side up. Insert a spatula or narrow knife between cake and edge of pan. When the tip of the spatula reaches the bottom, lift it out. Repeat this up-and-down motion all around the cake. Use this same motion to loosen the cake from the center tube. Invert the cake on a rack or plate and lift off the pan. Then turn the cake so it's right side up.

**Yesterday's cake:** Almost any cake tastes better the day it is made, but if well stored it will be delicious the second and even the third day. We have found that frosted cakes stay much fresher than unfrosted ones. Store both plain or frosted cakes in a "cake keeper," or cover them with a deep

16

bowl that will rest on the cake plate or tray without damaging the cake or frosting surface. To keep the unused portion of a cake fresher, we cover the cut surface of the cake with waxed paper or saran held in place with toothpicks inserted at an angle into the cake.

If a cake has a cream or whipped cream filling or topping, keep it refrigerated until serving time. Cover and store any uneaten portion in the refrigerator until ready to serve again.

Wrap fruit cakes tightly in waxed paper, aluminum foil, or plastic bags. We usually wrap fruit cakes while they are still very slightly warm — this makes them much more moist.

For suggestions for freezing all kinds of baked products, see Section 10.

*Desserts unlimited made with Swiss Chocolate Cake (p. 24).*
*This versatile cake bakes in a variety of pan sizes for filling*
*and frosting or for serving with scoops of ice cream.*

GENERAL FOODS
KITCHENS

SECTION 2

# Easy to Make Cakes

Chances are that the beginner's first sally into the world of flour and sifter, sugar and spice, pots and pans, will be a cake. For of all creations from the kitchen there is none that's a greater source of pleasure for the cook, beginner and old-timer alike, than a high, light, and handsome cake.

Basically cakes fall into two general categories; shortening-type cakes made with a fat of one kind or another, and sponge- or foam-types made without any shortening. Actually there are a few borderline cakes, such as the chiffon, but these are the exceptions that prove the rule.

*Shortening-type cakes:* These cakes are rich and tender with a fairly close, even grain and a soft crumb. They always contain fat (butter, margarine, or emulsified shortening) and a chemical leavening (baking powder and/or baking soda plus an acid) as well as sugar, flour, eggs, a liquid, and the flavoring. Methods of mixing are: *Conventional*—the fat is creamed with the sugar, then the eggs are added. The cake flour, which has been sifted with baking powder and salt, is added alternately with the liquid. *Mix-easy* — (a quick-mix method to be used only when the recipe has been specifically developed for this method) this method eliminates several time-consuming steps in mixing. Softened shortening is combined with sifted dry ingredients including sugar, cake flour, baking powder, and salt. The liquid ingredients and eggs are added, usually in two portions, then beaten for a

19

specified length of time or number of strokes. We have best results with this method when all the ingredients are at room temperature. The mixing and beating for both of these methods can be done either by hand or by electric mixer.

*Sponge- or foam-type cakes:* These are made without the addition of any fat if they are true sponge cakes. Some of them are made with baking powder, but they depend mainly upon air incorporated into beaten egg whites or yolks for leavening. It is quite important that the eggs be at room temperature since much greater volume is obtained with egg whites and yolks at room temperature. The way in which egg whites and yolks are combined with other ingredients is important in sponge-type cakes, too, for this same reason. If beaten egg whites are beaten into other ingredients incorporated air is lost — there goes your leavening. Unless otherwise directed, always use a folding motion (directions for folding are on page 9) to combine beaten egg whites and yolks with other ingredients.

Water or hot milk used in some sponge- or foam-type cakes creates steam as the cake bakes. This, too, acts as a leavening agent. Angel food cake is a foam-type cake that is made with egg whites only. Other sponge cakes can be made with egg yolks alone or with whole eggs.

*Chiffon cakes:* These are usually classified as sponge- or foam-type cakes, but they contain some of the best characteristics of both shortening- and sponge-type cakes. They have the high, airy lightness of an angel food and the tender richness of a shortening cake. The leavening for chiffon cakes is mostly air incorporated into eggs. Usually a small amount of chemical leavening is used, too. The fat used in these cakes is always liquid vegetable oil.

## SIZE UP YOUR CAKE

Certain cake pan sizes are ideal for particular cakes. These are the cake pans suggested in the recipe. Sometimes a cake will bake in other pans with, if not equally good results, almost as good results. The following chart gives suggested pan substitutions. But because every cake has a character of its own, this chart is not gospel. Never fill a pan more than *half full*. Make several halfway marks on all pans as your guide. If you've filled the pan or pans to the halfway mark and have a little batter left, use it for cupcakes. Cupcake pans should be filled one-half to two-thirds full.

The one hard and fast exception to the following chart of suggested pan substitutions is a pound cake. This regal cake demands baking either in a tube or loaf pan.

| If a cake bakes in . . . | It will also bake in . . . |
|---|---|
| 2) 8-inch layers | 2) thin 8x8x2-inch squares, 18 to 24) 2½-inch cupcake pans |
| 3) 8-inch layers | 2) 9x9x2-inch squares |
| 2) 9-inch layers | 2) 8x8x2-inch squares, 3) thin 8-inch layers, 1) 15x10x1-inch rectangle, 30) 2½-inch cupcake pans |
| 1) 8x8x2-inch square | 1) 9-inch layer |
| 2) 8x8x2-inch squares | 2) 9-inch layers, 1) 13x9x2-inch rectangle |
| 1) 9x9x2-inch square | 2) thin 8-inch layers |
| 2) 9x9x2-inch squares | 3) 8-inch layers |
| 1) 13x9x2-inch rectangle | 2) 9-inch layers, 2) 8x8x2-inch squares |
| 1) 12x8x2-inch rectangle | 2) 8-inch layers |
| 1) 9x5x3-inch loaf | 1) 9x9x2-inch square, 24 to 30) 2½-inch cupcake pans |
| 1) 8x4x3-inch loaf | 1) 8x8x2-inch square |
| 1) 9x3½-inch tube | 2) 9-inch layers, 24 to 30) 2½-inch cupcake pans |
| 1) 10x4-inch tube | 2) 9x5x3-inch loaves, 1) 13x9x2-inch rectangle, 2) 15x10x1-inch rectangles |

The recipes in this chapter are for simple, easy-to-make cakes. They contain the basic steps used to make all kinds of cakes. Follow directions and you'll find yourself serving the prettiest, best-tasting cakes imaginable.

### Easy Yellow Cake

*A big 9-inch layer cake made with only two eggs. Dress it up party-perfect with a luscious chocolate frosting.*

2¾ cups sifted Swans Down Cake Flour
3¼ teaspoons Calumet Baking Powder
1 teaspoon salt
1⅔ cups sugar
⅔ cup shortening (at room temperature)
1 cup plus 2 tablespoons milk*
1 teaspoon vanilla
2 eggs, unbeaten

* If butter or margarine is used, reduce milk to 1 cup.

Combine flour, baking powder, salt, and sugar in sifter. Stir shortening just to soften. Sift in dry ingredients. Add ¾ cup of the milk and the vanilla; mix until all flour is dampened. *Beat 2 minutes* at a low speed of electric mixer or 300 vigorous strokes by hand. Add eggs, remaining milk, and *beat 1 minute* longer in mixer or 150 strokes by hand.

Pour batter into two 9-inch layer pans or three 8-inch layer pans which have been lined on the bottoms with paper. Bake in moderate oven (350°F.) 25 to 30 minutes for 9-inch layers and 20 to 25 minutes for 8-inch layers. Or bake in a 13x9x2-inch pan for 35 to 40 minutes. Frost with Chocolate Cream Cheese Frosting (p. 59).

## Old-Fashioned Two-Egg Cake

*A lot can be said for this cake — it's not too rich but moist and flavorful.*

1¾ cups sifted Swans Down Cake Flour
2¼ teaspoons Calumet Baking Powder
½ teaspoon salt
½ cup shortening
1 cup plus 2 tablespoons sugar
2 eggs, unbeaten
¾ cup milk
1 teaspoon vanilla

Sift flour, baking powder, and salt together. Cream shortening thoroughly. Add sugar gradually and cream together until light and fluffy. Add eggs, one at a time, beating well after each. Then add flour alternately with milk, beating after each addition until smooth. Stir in vanilla.

Pour batter into two 8-inch layer pans which have been lined on bottoms with paper. Bake in moderate oven (375°F.) 25 to 30 minutes. Frost with Easy Chocolate Frosting (p. 56) or Coconut Cream Cheese Frosting (p. 59).

## Penny-Wise Cake

*The name speaks for itself — an economical, all-purpose cake. Try it as a Pineapple Upside-Down Cake.*

2 cups sifted Swans Down Cake Flour
2 teaspoons Calumet Baking Powder
¼ teaspoon salt
¼ cup shortening
1 cup sugar
1 egg, unbeaten
¾ cup milk
1 teaspoon vanilla

Sift flour, baking powder, and salt together. Cream shortening thoroughly. Add sugar gradually, and cream together well. Add egg and beat very thoroughly. Add flour alternately with milk, beating after each addition until smooth. Stir in vanilla.

Pour batter into a greased and floured 9x9x2-inch pan. Bake in moderate oven (350°F.) 35 minutes. Frost with Easy Chocolate Frosting (p. 56).

This cake may be also baked in 2 greased and floured 8-inch layer pans in moderate oven (375°F.) 25 minutes, or in a greased and floured 8x8x2-inch pan in moderate oven (350°F.) 50 minutes, or until done.

*Pineapple Upside-Down Cake.* Combine ¼ cup melted butter or margarine and ⅔ cup firmly packed brown sugar. Mix well and spread in 9x9x2-inch pan. Drain 1 can (8½ oz.) sliced pineapple and sprinkle 2 tablespoons of the juice over sugar mixture. Cut drained pineapple slices in quarters and arrange over sugar mixture. Sprinkle with ½ cup chopped nuts. Prepare Penny-Wise Cake batter as directed. Pour into pan over pineapple. Bake in moderate oven (350°F.) 45 to 50 minutes. Let cake cool in pan 5 minutes, then invert pan on serving dish. Let stand 1 minute before removing pan. Serve warm. Makes about 9 servings.

## Red Devil's Food Cake

*A cake fit for angels, too. This little layer cake has that distinctive red-chocolate color and an outstanding flavor.*

1½ cups sifted Swans Down Cake Flour
¾ teaspoon salt
¾ teaspoon baking soda
1¼ cups sugar
½ cup shortening (at room temperature)
⅔ cup water
2 squares Baker's Unsweetened
  Chocolate, melted
2 eggs, unbeaten
1 teaspoon vanilla

Combine flour, salt, soda, and sugar in sifter. Stir shortening just to soften. Sift in dry ingredients. Add water and mix until all flour is dampened. Then *beat*

*2 minutes* at a low speed of electric mixer or 300 vigorous strokes by hand. Add chocolate, eggs, and vanilla and *beat 1 minute* longer in mixer or 150 strokes by hand.

Pour batter into 9x9x2-inch pan or two 8-inch layer pans which have been lined on bottoms with paper. Bake in moderate oven (350°F.) 40 to 45 minutes for the square cake or 25 to 30 minutes for the 8-inch layers. Frost with Sea Foam Frosting or Easy Chocolate Frosting (p. 56).

## Sugarplum Spice Cake

*A sweet, spicy cake with a delicate, feathery-soft texture. Sugarplum Frosting makes a perfect flavor mate.*

2½ cups sifted Swans Down Cake Flour
1 teaspoon Calumet Baking Powder
1 teaspoon baking soda
¾ teaspoon salt
¾ teaspoon cinnamon
½ teaspoon cloves
1 cup granulated sugar
½ cup shortening (at room temperature)
⅔ cup firmly packed brown sugar
1 cup plus 2 tablespoons buttermilk*
2 eggs, unbeaten

* If butter or margarine is used, reduce buttermilk to 1 cup.

Combine flour, baking powder, soda, salt, spices, and granulated sugar in sifter. Stir shortening just to soften. Sift in dry ingredients. Add brown sugar and buttermilk and mix until all flour is dampened. Then *beat 2 minutes* at a low speed of electric mixer or 300 vigorous strokes by hand. Add eggs and *beat 1 minute* longer in mixer or 150 strokes by hand.

Pour batter into two 9-inch layer pans which have been lined on bottoms with paper. Bake in moderate oven (375°F.) 25 to 30 minutes. Cool. Frost with Sugarplum Frosting (p. 57).

This cake may also be baked in a 13x9x2-inch pan about 40 minutes or in a 9x9x2-inch pan about 50 minutes.

*Chip-Nut Cocoa Cake (p. 25) makes a fine selection for picnics and other "carry-all" occasions.*

## San Antonio Cocoa Cake

*A fine, mild flavored cocoa cake that's very tender and moist. Frost it with a soft fluffy frosting.*

½ cup Baker's Cocoa
1¾ cups sugar
1½ cups buttermilk or sour milk
2¼ cups sifted Swans Down Cake Flour
1 teaspoon baking soda
1 teaspoon salt
½ cup shortening
2 eggs, unbeaten
1 teaspoon vanilla

Combine cocoa and ½ cup of the sugar in small bowl. Add ½ cup of the buttermilk and blend until smooth.

Sift flour, soda, and salt together. Cream shortening thoroughly. Add remaining 1¼ cups sugar gradually, and cream together until light and fluffy. Add eggs, one at a time, beating well after each. Add flour alternately with the remaining 1 cup buttermilk, beating after each addition until smooth. Add vanilla and cocoa mixture and blend.

Pour batter into two 9-inch layer pans which have been lined on bottoms with paper. Bake in moderate oven (350°F.) 30 to 35 minutes. Frost with Fluffy Seven Minute Frosting (p. 55), Snowy Boiled Frosting, or Sea Foam Frosting (p. 56).

23

## Easy Gold Cake

*A golden-hued cake that's unusual since only 3 egg yolks are needed.*

2¼ cups sifted Swans Down Cake Flour
2½ teaspoons Calumet Baking Powder
¾ teaspoon salt
½ cup shortening
1 cup sugar
3 egg yolks
1 cup plus 2 tablespoons milk*
1 teaspoon vanilla

* If butter or margarine is used, decrease milk to 1 cup.

Sift flour, baking powder, and salt together. Cream shortening thoroughly. Add sugar gradually and cream together until light and fluffy. Add egg yolks and beat thoroughly. Add flour alternately with milk, beating after each addition until smooth. Stir in vanilla.

Pour batter into two 8-inch layer pans which have been lined on bottoms with paper. Bake in moderate oven (375°F.) 25 minutes, or until done.

Frost with Fluffy Butter or Chocolate Butter Frosting (p. 59).

## Swiss Chocolate Cake

*A moist, milk chocolate cake. "Frost" with Meringue Topping for a picnic special that's easily transported.*

1¾ cups sifted Swans Down Cake Flour
2 teaspoons Calumet Baking Powder
¼ teaspoon baking soda
1 teaspoon salt
1½ cups sugar
½ cup shortening (at room temperature)
1¼ cups undiluted evaporated milk
2 eggs, unbeaten
1 teaspoon vanilla
2 squares Baker's Unsweetened Chocolate, melted
¼ teaspoon red food coloring, optional

Combine flour, baking powder, soda, salt, and sugar in sifter. Stir shortening just to soften. Sift in dry ingredients. Add 1 cup of the milk and mix until all flour is dampened. *Beat 2 minutes*

*Dress up Old-Fashioned Two-Egg Cake (p. 22) with Coconut Cream Cheese Frosting (p. 59) and toasted flakes of coconut.*

at a low speed of electric mixer or 300 vigorous strokes by hand. Add eggs, vanilla, melted chocolate, food coloring, and remaining milk. *Beat 1 minute* longer in mixer or 150 strokes by hand.

Pour batter into two 9-inch layer pans or three 8-inch layer pans which have been lined on the bottoms with paper. Bake in moderate oven (350°F.) 25 to 30 minutes for 9-inch layers and 20 to 25 minutes for 8-inch layers. Frost with Sea Foam Frosting (p. 56) or Chocolate Fudge Frosting (p. 58).

This cake may also be baked in two 8x8x2-inch pans in moderate oven (350°F.) 30 to 35 minutes, or in 13x-9x2-inch pan 35 to 40 minutes. Frost with Meringue Topping (p. 58).

*Paisley Chocolate Cake.* Prepare Swiss Chocolate Cake; pour batter in two 9-inch layer pans as directed. Melt 2 squares Baker's Unsweetened Chocolate; pour in a circle on top of batter in both pans, about 1 inch from rims. With a rubber scraper or a spatula swirl chocolate in continuous circles through the batter, once around each pan. Bake as directed. Cool. Split each layer horizontally. Spread Peppermint Topping (p. 61) between layers; leave top unfrosted. Chill until serving time.

## Favorite Butterscotch Cake

*The wonderfully rich brown-sugar flavor of this cake is echoed in a caramel fudge frosting.*

2 cups sifted Swans Down Cake Flour
1½ teaspoons Calumet Baking Powder
½ teaspoon baking soda
1 teaspoon salt
½ cup shortening
1⅓ cups firmly packed brown sugar
1 cup minus 2 tablespoons milk*
1½ teaspoons vanilla
2 eggs, unbeaten

*If butter is used, reduce milk to ¾ cup.

Combine flour, baking powder, soda, and salt in sifter. Stir shortening just to soften. Sift in flour mixture. Add brown sugar. Add the milk and vanilla and mix until all flour is dampened. *Beat 2 minutes* at a low speed of electric mixer or 300 vigorous strokes by hand. Add eggs; *beat 1 minute* longer in mixer or 150 strokes by hand.

Pour batter into two 8-inch layer pans which have been lined on bottoms with paper. Bake in moderate oven (375°F.) 20 to 25 minutes. Frost with Quick Caramel Frosting (p. 57) or Sea Foam Frosting (p. 56).

## Chip-Nut Cocoa Cake

*As much bar cooky as it is cake. It's quite rich and has a built-in frosting.*

1 cup finely chopped dates
1 cup boiling water
1 teaspoon baking soda
1¾ cups sifted flour
¼ cup Baker's Cocoa
½ teaspoon salt
1 cup shortening
1 cup sugar
2 eggs, beaten
1 teaspoon vanilla
½ cup chopped nuts, optional
1 cup (6-oz. package) Baker's Semi-Sweet Chocolate Chips

Mix together dates, water, and soda. Cool. Sift flour, cocoa, and salt together. Cream shortening thoroughly. Add sugar gradually and cream together until light and fluffy. Add the eggs and vanilla; beat well. Then add flour alternately with the date mixture, beating after each addition.

Pour batter into a 15x10x1-inch pan which has been greased on the bottom. Sprinkle nuts and chips over top and press lightly into batter. Bake in moderate oven (350°F.) 25 to 30 minutes. Cool and cut in bars. Makes 3 dozen. *Note:* Batter may also be poured into a 13x9x2-inch pan which has been greased on the bottom. Bake in moderate oven (350°F.) 40 to 45 minutes. Makes about 18 squares. Serve plain or with ice cream.

## Devil's Food Cupcakes

*Delicious little chocolate cakes made the mix-easy way.*

1 cup sifted Swans Down Cake Flour
½ teaspoon salt
½ teaspoon baking soda
¼ cup Baker's Cocoa
¾ cup sugar
¼ cup shortening (at room temperature)
⅔ cup buttermilk*
½ teaspoon vanilla
1 egg plus 1 egg yolk, unbeaten

*If butter or margarine is used, reduce buttermilk to ½ cup.

Combine flour, salt, soda, cocoa, and sugar in sifter. Stir shortening just to soften. Sift in dry ingredients. Add half of the buttermilk and the vanilla; mix until all flour is dampened. Then *beat 2 minutes* at a low speed of electric mixer or 300 vigorous strokes by hand. Add remaining buttermilk, egg, and egg yolk and *beat 1 minute* longer in mixer or 150 strokes by hand.

Spoon batter into muffin pans, which have been lined with paper cupcake liners. Fill only half full. Bake in moderate oven (350°F.) 25 to 30 minutes. Makes about 18 medium cupcakes.

## Featherweight Cupcakes

*These fine textured cakes stay fresher and are more attractive when baked in fluted paper cups.*

2 cups sifted Swans Down Cake Flour
2¼ teaspoons Calumet Baking Powder
½ teaspoon salt
½ cup shortening
1¼ cups sugar*
2 eggs, unbeaten
1 cup milk*
1 teaspoon vanilla

* If butter or margarine is used, decrease sugar to 1 cup and milk to 1 cup minus 2 tablespoons.

Sift flour, baking powder, and salt together. Cream shortening thoroughly. Add sugar gradually and cream together until light and fluffy. Add eggs and beat thoroughly. Add flour alternately with milk, mixing after each addition just until blended. Stir in vanilla.

Fill muffin pans, which have been lined with paper cupcake liners, one-half full. Bake in a moderate oven (375°F.) for 20 to 25 minutes. Makes about 2½ dozen cupcakes. Frost with a butter cream or fluffy frosting.

## Crumb Cake

*A sweet, crumb-topped cake that's good for tea and snacks. Serve warm!*

¼ cup sugar
¾ cup flour
½ teaspoon cinnamon
Dash of salt
¼ cup butter or margarine, melted
½ teaspoon vanilla
¼ cup shortening
⅓ cup sugar
1 egg
1 cup sifted flour
1½ teaspoons Calumet Baking Powder
¼ teaspoon salt
½ cup milk
½ teaspoon vanilla

Combine ¼ cup sugar, ¾ cup flour, the cinnamon, and a dash of salt; stir to blend. Combine butter and ½ teaspoon vanilla. Add to flour mixture about 1 tablespoon at a time, tossing with a fork until mixture forms crumbs.

Cream shortening with ⅓ cup sugar until fluffy. Add egg and blend. Sift 1 cup flour, the baking powder, and ¼ teaspoon salt together. Then combine milk and ½ teaspoon vanilla. Add flour alternately with milk to egg mixture, mixing after each addition until smooth.

Pour batter into a greased 8x8x2-inch pan. Sprinkle the crumbs evenly over batter. Bake in a moderate oven (375°F.) for 30 minutes. Serve warm.

*Serve Pineapple Upside-Down Cake (p. 22) for informal parties and get-togethers and family suppers.*

## Gingerbread

*An old-fashioned cake with a superb blend of molasses and spice flavors.*

1⅔ cups sifted Swans Down Cake Flour
1 teaspoon Calumet Baking Powder
¾ teaspoon baking soda
½ teaspoon salt
¼ cup sugar
½ teaspoon cinnamon
½ teaspoon ginger
¼ teaspoon cloves
¼ cup shortening (at room temperature)
½ cup water
½ cup molasses
1 egg, unbeaten

Combine flour, baking powder, soda, salt, sugar, and spices in sifter. Stir shortening just to soften. Sift in dry ingredients. Combine water and molasses. Add ¾ cup of the liquid and mix until all flour is dampened. Then *beat 2 minutes* at a low speed of electric mixer or 300 vigorous strokes by hand. Add remaining liquid and the egg and *beat 1 minute* longer in mixer or 150 strokes by hand.

Pour batter into a 9x9x2-inch pan, or an 8x8x2-inch pan which has been greased on the bottom and lightly dusted with flour. Bake in moderate oven (350°F.) 25 to 30 minutes for 9-inch cake and 30 to 35 minutes for 8-inch cake. Serve warm with butter, applesauce, or whipped cream.

*Note:* For an extra large gingerbread, double all ingredients and bake in 13x9x2-inch pan in moderate oven (350°F.) about 40 minutes.

## Hot Milk Sponge Cake

*A classic among cakes — simple and economical to make. Serve it as a tuck-in-treat for lunchboxes.*

2 cups sifted Swans Down Cake Flour
2 teaspoons Calumet Baking Powder
½ teaspoon salt
4 eggs, unbeaten
2 cups sugar
2 teaspoons vanilla or 1 tablespoon
 grated orange rind
1 cup milk
2 tablespoons butter or margarine

Sift flour, baking powder, and salt together. Beat eggs in large deep bowl until very thick and light — about 5 minutes. Gradually beat in sugar. Add vanilla. Add flour to egg mixture, a small amount at a time, blending by hand or at low speed of electric mixer. Bring milk and butter just to a boil. Very quickly stir into the flour mixture, blending thoroughly. (Batter will be thin.) Pour quickly into a 13x9x2-inch pan which has been greased and floured on bottom only. Bake at once in moderate oven (350°F.) for 30 to 35 minutes. Cool slightly, then spread with Broiled Coconut Topping. Serve warm.

*Note:* For a smaller cake, divide all ingredients in half and pour in an 8x8x2-inch pan which has been greased and floured on bottom only. Bake in moderate oven (350°F.) 25 to 30 minutes.

**Broiled Coconut Topping.** Cream ¼ cup butter and ¾ cup firmly packed brown sugar together. Add 1½ tablespoons milk and beat until smooth. Then mix in ¾ cup Baker's Angel Flake Coconut. Spread on cake in pan and broil for about 3 minutes, or until coconut is lightly toasted.

## Chocolate Chiffon Cake

*A deep, dark chocolate cake that's melt-in-your-mouth tender. Serve it unfrosted to show off the textured top.*

1¾ cups sifted Swans Down Cake Flour
1 teaspoon baking soda
2 cups sugar
⅔ cup Baker's Cocoa
2 teaspoons cream of tartar
½ cup salad oil
7 egg yolks, unbeaten
1 cup minus 2 tablespoons water
1 teaspoon vanilla
1 cup (8 to 10) egg whites (at room temperature)
1½ teaspoons salt
½ teaspoon cream of tartar

Sift flour, soda, sugar, cocoa, and 2 teaspoons cream of tartar together. Combine oil, egg yolks, water, and vanilla in mixing bowl. Add sifted ingredients and beat about ½ minute at low speed of electric mixer or 75 strokes by hand.

Combine egg whites, salt, and ½ teaspoon cream of tartar in large bowl. Beat at high speed of electric mixer or with sturdy egg beater until mixture will stand in *very stiff* peaks — about 5 minutes. (The egg whites should be beaten stiffer than for meringue or angel food cake. Do not underbeat.) Fold egg whites thoroughly into batter with large spoon. (Do not stir or beat.)

Pour batter into ungreased 10-inch tube pan. Bake in moderate oven (350°F.) 1 hour and 10 to 15 minutes. Cool cake in pan, upside down, 1 to 2 hours. Then loosen from sides and center tube with spatula or knife. Serve cake with plain or Cocoa Whipped Cream (p. 60) or with ice cream.

## Angel Food Cake

*The classical snowy-white cake with a moist macaroon top.*

1 cup plus 2 tablespoons sifted Swans Down Cake Flour
1½ cups sifted sugar
1¼ cups (10 to 12) egg whites (at room temperature)
¼ teaspoon salt
1¼ teaspoons cream of tartar
1 teaspoon vanilla
¼ teaspoon almond extract

Sift flour and ½ cup of the sugar together. Combine egg whites, salt, cream of tartar, and flavorings in large bowl. Beat with flat wire whip, sturdy egg beater, or at high speed of electric mixer until soft peaks form. Add remaining 1 cup of sugar gradually, 4 tablespoons at a time, beating well after each addition. When beating by hand, beat 25 strokes after each addition.

Sift in flour mixture in four additions, folding in with 15 fold-over strokes each time and turning bowl frequently. (Do not stir or beat.) After last addition, use 10 to 20 extra folding strokes. Pour batter into ungreased 9- or 10-inch tube pan. Bake in moderate oven (375°F.) 35 to 40 minutes for 9-inch cake and 30 to 35 minutes for 10-inch cake, or until cake springs back when pressed lightly. Cool cake in pan, upside down 1 to 2 hours. Then loosen from sides and center tube with knife and gently pull out cake. Serve plain, sprinkle with confectioners' sugar, or frost with Butter Cream Frosting (p. 57).

**Sweet Chocolate Swirl Cake.** Prepare Angel Food Cake as directed. Pour ¼ of batter into ungreased 10-inch tube pan, spreading smoothly. Grate ⅔ bar (4 sections) Baker's German's Sweet Chocolate. Sprinkle about ⅓ of grated chocolate through coarse sieve over batter in pan. Repeat, alternating layers of batter and grated chocolate (4 layers of batter, 3 of chocolate). Bake and cool as directed. Frost with Sweet Chocolate Glaze (p. 60), Chocolate Butter Cream Frosting (p. 57), or sprinkle with confectioners' sugar.

*Make Easy Yellow Cake (p. 21) party perfect with luscious Chocolate Cream Cheese Frosting (p. 59).*

*A fitting tribute to the sixteenth year — a fesitve Sweet 16 Cake made with Crown Cake (p. 35) and frosted with tinted Fluffy Seven Minute Frosting (p. 55).*

SECTION 3

# The Party Cake

The cakes in this chapter are lofty, elegant, dream cakes — cakes to win new laurels, to grace that very special occasion. There are triple decker birthday cakes ablaze with candles, festive marble cakes swirled through and through with rich chocolate, feather light cake rolls filled and frosted to perfection, and big lovely luscious cakes that will walk away with first prize in any contest.

These cakes are basically the same shortening- and sponge-type cakes found in the preceding chapter — a little more difficult perhaps, in that they have additional steps or techniques to master. But we think they are well worth it. Here again emulsified shortening has been used in all recipes unless otherwise specified.

When one frosting is particularly suited to a cake, we have suggested it. This in no way implies it is the only frosting that will be good; your choice is the final one.

31

*Transform Heavenly White Cake (p. 32) into a birthday special with Fluffy Seven Minute Frosting (p. 55) and mounds of fluffy white coconut.*

## Heavenly White Cake

*A soft, downy textured cake that tastes good with about any kind of frosting.*

2¾ cups sifted Swans Down Cake Flour
4 teaspoons Calumet Baking Powder
¾ teaspoon salt
4 egg whites
1½ cups sugar
¾ cup shortening
1 cup plus 2 tablespoons milk
1 teaspoon vanilla
½ teaspoon almond extract

Sift flour, baking powder, and salt together. Beat egg whites until foamy. Add ½ cup of the sugar gradually and continue beating only until meringue will hold up in soft peaks. Cream shortening thoroughly. Add remaining 1 cup sugar gradually and cream together until light and fluffy. Add flour alternately with milk, beating after each addition until smooth. Mix in flavorings. Then add meringue and beat thoroughly into batter.

Pour batter into two 9-inch layer pans or three 8-inch layer pans which have been lined on bottoms with paper. Bake in moderate oven (350°F.) 30 to 35 minutes for 9-inch cakes and 25 to 30 minutes for 8-inch cakes. Frost with a butter cream or fluffy frosting.

**Caterer's Cakes.** Prepare Heavenly White Cake batter as directed. Spread it in a 15x10x1-inch pan which has

32

been lined on bottom with paper. Bake in moderate oven (350°F.) 30 to 35 minutes. Cool 10 minutes in pan, then remove to rack to cool thoroughly. Invert cooled cake on a large board. Remove paper and rub off crumbs. With a long sharp knife, trim edges and cut cake into four 7 x 4½-inch rectangles. Frost, bottom side up, using white or tinted frosting on each section to give an attractive assortment. Then dip knife in hot water and cut quarter sections into squares, diamonds, rectangles, and triangles, as desired. Decorate with bits of candied fruit, nuts, tiny colored candies, coconut, or melted chocolate.

## German's
## Sweet Chocolate Cake

*This cake is high in sugar, high in fat, and a bit temperamental — but it has no equal for delicacy and good flavor! A fragile, crusty top is characteristic.*

1 package (¼ pound) Baker's German's Sweet Chocolate
½ cup boiling water
1 cup butter or margarine
2 cups sugar
4 egg yolks, unbeaten
1 teaspoon vanilla
2½ cups sifted Swans Down Cake Flour
1 teaspoon baking soda
½ teaspoon salt
1 cup buttermilk
4 egg whites, stiffly beaten

Melt chocolate in ½ cup of boiling water. Cool. Cream butter and sugar together until light and fluffy. Add egg yolks, one at a time, beating after each. Add vanilla and melted chocolate and mix until blended. Sift flour, soda, and salt together. Add flour to the chocolate mixture alternately with buttermilk, beating after each addition until smooth. Fold in stiffly beaten egg whites.

Pour batter into three 8- or 9-inch layer pans which have been lined on bottoms with paper. Bake in moderate

oven (350°F.) for 35 to 40 minutes for 8-inch layers and 30 to 35 minutes for 9-inch layers. Cool. Frost with Coconut Pecan Frosting and Filling (p. 59).

This cake may also be baked in two 8- or 9-inch square pans which have been lined on bottoms with paper. Bake in moderate oven (350°F.) for 45 to 50 minutes for 8-inch squares or 40 to 45 minutes for 9-inch squares.

## Three-Layer Fudge Cake

*A big, handsome cake to serve a crowd. Chocolate custard added to the batter makes a moist, fine grained cake.*

5 eggs
4 squares Baker's Unsweetened Chocolate
2½ cups sugar
1¾ cups milk
¾ cup shortening
1½ teaspoons vanilla
3 cups sifted Swans Down Cake Flour
1½ teaspoons baking soda
¾ teaspoon salt

Beat 1 egg and combine with the chocolate, 1 cup of the sugar, and ¾ cup of the milk in a saucepan. Cook, stirring constantly, over low heat until chocolate melts and mixture thickens. Cool to room temperature.

Cream shortening thoroughly. Gradually add remaining 1½ cups sugar and cream together until light and fluffy. Add vanilla. Then add remaining eggs, one at a time, beating well after each addition. Sift flour, soda, and salt together. Add to shortening mixture alternately with remaining 1 cup of milk, beating after each addition until smooth. Blend in chocolate mixture.

Pour into three 9-inch layer pans lined on bottoms with paper. Bake in moderate oven (350°F.) for 30 to 35 minutes, or until cake springs back when lightly pressed. Cool layers. Frost with Sea Foam Frosting (p. 56).

## Lemon Gold Cake

*The liquid measurement in this cake may seem strange, but that's exactly what it takes — measure carefully!*

2½ cups sifted Swans Down Cake Flour
2½ teaspoons Calumet Baking Powder
½ teaspoon salt
½ cup shortening
1 tablespoon grated lemon rind*
1¾ cups sugar
6 egg yolks, unbeaten
1 cup plus 3 tablespoons milk

* One teaspoon lemon extract plus ½ teaspoon vanilla may be substituted for the lemon rind.

Sift flour, baking powder, and salt together. Cream shortening and lemon rind together. Add sugar gradually and cream together until light and fluffy. Add egg yolks, one at a time, beating thoroughly after each. Then add flour alternately with milk, beating after each addition until smooth.

Pour batter into two 9-inch layer pans which have been lined on bottoms with paper. Bake in moderate oven (350°F.) 30 to 35 minutes. Or bake in a 13x9x2-inch pan 40 to 45 minutes. Frost with Lemon Butter Cream Frosting (p. 57).

## Sweet Chocolate-Apricot Torte

*Similar to the famous Austrian torte — thin (and we mean thin) rich chocolate layers frosted with apricot cream.*

¼ cup water
1 package (¼ pound) Baker's German's Sweet Chocolate
6 egg yolks
½ cup sugar
¼ cup butter (at room temperature)
6 egg whites
½ cup sifted flour

Combine water and chocolate in a small saucepan. Place over low heat and stir until chocolate is melted and mixture is smooth. Cool. Beat egg yolks; gradually add sugar, 2 tablespoons at a time, beating until lemon colored and thick. Add butter and beat until smooth. Then add cooled chocolate mixture and beat until smooth and creamy. Beat egg whites until stiff peaks form. Gradually fold in flour; then fold into chocolate mixture.

Grease two 8-inch layer pans on bottoms, then line with paper and grease again. Pour about ¼ of batter (about 1 cup) into each pan. (Chill remaining batter while first 2 layers bake.) Bake in a slow oven (325°F.) for 15 minutes. Cool 5 minutes and then turn out onto rack. Remove paper carefully and continue to cool on rack. Repeat with remaining batter. Fill layers and frost top of cake with Apricot Whipped Cream. Makes 12 servings.

*Apricot Whipped Cream.* Whip 1 cup heavy cream until stiff peaks form. Carefully fold in ¾ cup apricot jam. Makes 2½ cups.

## Light Coconut Fruit Cake

*A light, delicate fruit cake with wisps of coconut lending an unusually good flavor and texture.*

2 cups (7-oz. package) Baker's Fine-Grated Coconut
2 pounds mixed candied fruit
1 pound pitted dates, cut in small pieces
1 pound white raisins, washed and dried
½ pound candied cherries, cut
½ pound walnuts, chopped
2½ cups sifted flour
½ pound butter or margarine
1¼ cups sugar
6 eggs, unbeaten
½ teaspoon Calumet Baking Powder
Dash of salt
1 teaspoon vanilla

Combine coconut, fruits, and nuts with ½ cup of the flour. Mix well. Cream butter thoroughly. Add sugar gradually and cream together until light and fluffy. Add eggs, one at a time, beating well after each. Sift remaining flour, the baking powder, and salt together. Add to cream mixture; blend well. Blend in vanilla and fruit mixture.

Line bottoms of three 9x5x3-inch loaf pans with heavy brown paper. Spoon batter into pans up to 1 inch from top. Bake in slow oven (275°F.) for 1 hour; then bake at 300°F. for ½ to 1 hour longer, or until cake tester inserted in center comes out clean. Makes 7 pounds of cake.

This cake may be served the same day as baked, or stored in tightly covered container for later use. For long storage, wrap in cheesecloth soaked in grape or other fruit juice. Keep in tightly covered container.

## Crown Cake

*A pound-cake-like cake but very easy to make. Its top will split slightly in typical pound-cake fashion.*

3 cups sifted Swans Down Cake Flour
2 teaspoons Calumet Baking Powder
1½ teaspoons salt
1¾ cups sugar
1 cup shortening (at room temperature)
¾ cup milk*
¾ teaspoon orange or almond extract
3 eggs and 1 egg yolk, unbeaten

* If butter or margarine is used, decrease milk to ½ cup.

Combine flour, baking powder, salt, and sugar in sifter. Stir shortening just to soften. Sift in dry ingredients. Add milk and extract and mix until all flour is dampened. Then *beat 2 minutes* at a low speed of electric mixer or 300 vigorous strokes by hand. Add eggs and egg yolk and *beat 1 minute* longer in mixer or 150 strokes by hand.

Pour batter into a 9-inch tube pan which has been greased and lightly floured on bottom, sides, and tube. Bake in moderate oven (375°F.) 50 to 55 minutes, or until done. Cool in pan about 15 minutes. Then remove

from pan and cool right side up on rack. Sprinkle with confectioners' sugar or frost with Orange or Lemon Butter Cream Frosting (p. 57).
*Note:* This cake may also be baked in two 8- or 9-inch square pans which have been greased and lightly floured on the bottoms only. Bake in moderate oven (375°F.) for 25 to 30 minutes. Cool as directed above.

## Pound Cake

*Cream the butter, then cream it some more — that's the secret of a good pound cake. Beat the eggs in thoroughly — one by one.*

2¼ cups sifted Swans Down Cake Flour
1 teaspoon Calumet Baking Powder
½ teaspoon salt
1 cup butter or margarine
1¼ cups sugar
1¼ teaspoons vanilla
¼ teaspoon mace
4 eggs, unbeaten
¼ cup milk

Sift flour, baking powder, and salt together. Cream butter until *very soft and fluffy.* Add sugar, 2 tablespoons at a time, creaming thoroughly after each addition. (Beat at least 10 minutes in mixer — longer by hand.) Add vanilla and mace, blending well. Beat in eggs, one at a time, beating thoroughly after each. Add flour mixture alternately with the milk, beating after each addition until smooth.

Pour batter into a 9x5x3-inch pan or 9-inch tube pan which has been lined on the bottom with paper. Bake in a slow oven (325°F.) 1 hour and 15 to 20 minutes, or until cake tests done. Cool about 15 minutes in pan. Then turn out, remove paper, and turn right side up to cool thoroughly. Serve plain or with fruit and ice cream.
*Note:* Cake slices better and is more moist when stored overnight. Wrap tightly in saran or in aluminum foil.

*Pick up the delicate lemon flavor in Fantasy Sponge Cake (p. 39) with a Lemon Butter Glaze (p. 60).*

## Prune Spice Cake

*An outstanding combination of prune and spice flavors in a moist, luscious three-layer cake.*

3 cups sifted Swans Down Cake Flour
2½ teaspoons Calumet Baking Powder
1 teaspoon baking soda
1 teaspoon salt
1 teaspoon cinnamon
1 teaspoon nutmeg
½ teaspoon mace
¾ cup shortening
2 cups sugar
3 eggs
1 teaspoon vanilla
1½ cups drained coarsely
    chopped prunes*
1¼ cups buttermilk

* Use canned stewed prunes or well-cooked dried prunes, which have stood overnight in the juice.

Sift flour, baking powder, soda, salt, and spices together. Cream shortening. Add sugar gradually and cream to-

36

gether until light and fluffy. Add eggs, one at a time, beating well after each. Add vanilla and prunes. Add flour alternately with buttermilk, beating well after each addition.

Pour batter into three 9-inch layer pans or two 9x9x2-inch pans which have been lined on bottoms with paper. Bake in a moderate oven (350°F.) 30 to 35 minutes for round pans and 35 to 40 minutes for square pans. Cool. Frost with Butter Cream or Coffee Butter Cream Frosting (p. 57).

## Old-fashioned Spice Cake

*This is a very soft, velvety cake with a dash of black pepper (that's right) to "pick up" the spice flavor.*

2¼ cups sifted Swans Down Cake Flour
1 teaspoon Calumet Baking Powder
1 teaspoon salt
¾ teaspoon baking soda
¾ teaspoon cloves
¾ teaspoon cinnamon
Pinch of black pepper
¾ cup shortening
¾ cup firmly packed brown sugar
1 cup granulated sugar
3 eggs, unbeaten
1 cup plus 2 tablespoons buttermilk*
1 teaspoon vanilla

* If butter or margarine is used, decrease buttermilk to 1 cup.

Sift flour, baking powder, salt, soda, spices, and pepper together. Cream shortening thoroughly. Gradually add sugars and cream together until light and fluffy. Add eggs, one at a time, beating well after each. Add flour alternately with buttermilk. Beat after each addition until smooth. Add vanilla.

Pour batter into three 8-inch layer pans or two 9-inch layer pans which have been lined on bottoms with paper. Bake in moderate oven (350°F.) 25 to 30 minutes for the 8-inch layers and 30 to 35 minutes for the 9-inch layers. Frost with a butter cream frosting.

## German's
## Chocolate Filbert Cake

*A fine, milk chocolate nut cake that stays moist and fresh tasting for days. A bit costly — but worth every penny.*

1 package (¼ pound) Baker's German's Sweet Chocolate
2¾ cups sifted Swans Down Cake Flour
2 teaspoons Calumet Baking Powder
½ teaspoon salt
1 cup butter or margarine
1⅔ cups sugar
4 egg yolks, unbeaten
1 teaspoon vanilla
1 cup milk
1 cup finely chopped filberts or walnuts
4 egg whites

Melt chocolate over hot water; then cool. Sift flour, baking powder, and salt together. Cream butter thoroughly. Add sugar gradually and cream together until light and fluffy. Add egg yolks, one at a time, beating well after each. Blend in melted chocolate and vanilla. Add flour mixture alternately with milk, beating after each addition until smooth. Fold in nuts. Beat egg whites until stiff peaks form, then fold into batter.

Pour batter into a well-greased and floured 10-inch tube pan or a 13x9x2-inch pan. Bake in moderate oven (350°F.) 1 hour and 10 to 15 minutes for tube pan and 50 to 55 minutes for 13x9x2-inch pan. Cool 15 minutes; then remove from pan and cool thoroughly on rack. "Frost" tube cake with confectioners' sugar. Top 13x9-inch cake with Broiled Coconut Topping (p. 28).

*A superb chocolate cake! Frost* German's *Sweet Chocolate Cake (p. 33) with Coconut Pecan Frosting and Filling (p. 59).*

## Black and Gold Marble Cake

*Chocolate rippling through gold cake makes a pretty pattern — a cake to tempt the eye as well as treat the taste.*

2 squares Baker's Unsweetened
    Chocolate
3 tablespoons hot water
3 tablespoons sugar
2½ cups sifted Swans Down Cake Flour
2½ teaspoons Calumet Baking Powder
1 teaspoon salt
½ teaspoon baking soda
1⅔ cups sugar
¾ cup shortening (at room temperature)
1 cup plus 2 tablespoons buttermilk*
1 teaspoon vanilla
3 eggs, unbeaten

\* If butter or margarine is used, reduce buttermilk to 1 cup minus 2 tablespoons.

Melt chocolate; add hot water and 3 tablespoons sugar. Stir until smooth.

Combine flour, baking powder, salt, soda, and 1⅔ cups sugar in sifter. Stir shortening just to soften. Sift in dry ingredients. Add buttermilk and vanilla and mix until all flour is dampened. Then *beat 2 minutes* at low speed of electric mixer or 300 vigorous strokes by hand. Add eggs and *beat 1 minute* longer in mixer or 150 strokes by hand. Pour half of batter into a bowl, add chocolate mixture and blend well.

Line two 9-inch layer pans on bottoms with paper. Put large spoonfuls of batters into pans, alternating plain and chocolate mixtures. Then with a knife, cut through batter once in a wide zigzag course to marble. Bake in a moderate oven (350°F.) for 30 to 35 minutes. Frost with Fluffy Chocolate Butter Frosting (p. 60).

*Split layers of Crown Cake (p. 35), then fill and frost with Fluffy Chocolate Frosting (p. 56). Compound the chocolate interest by swirling melted chocolate over the top.*

38

## Orange Juice Cake

*Not just a yellow cake with an orange filling, but a true orange cake with a sparkling flavor and fine texture.*

3 cups sifted Swans Down Cake Flour
3¼ teaspoons Calumet Baking Powder
¾ teaspoon salt
½ teaspoon baking soda
⅔ cup shortening
2½ teaspoons grated orange rind
1⅔ cups sugar
2 eggs, unbeaten
½ cup milk*
1 cup orange juice

\* If butter or margarine is used, decrease milk to ¼ cup.

Sift flour, baking powder, salt, and soda together. Cream shortening and grated orange rind thoroughly. Gradually add sugar and cream together until light and fluffy. Add eggs, one at a time, beating thoroughly after each. Then add flour alternately with milk first, then with orange juice, beating after each addition until smooth.

Pour batter into two 9-inch or three 8-inch layer pans lined on bottoms with paper. Bake in moderate oven (375°F.) 25 minutes for 9-inch layers or 20 to 25 minutes for 8-inch layers. Frost with Orange Butter Frosting (p. 57).

## Daffodil Cake

*This is a high, light, and lovely silver and gold cake.*

1¼ cups sifted Swans Down Cake Flour
1½ cups sifted sugar
1¼ cups (10 to 12) egg whites (at room temperature)
¼ teaspoon salt
1½ teaspoons cream of tartar
½ teaspoon vanilla
4 egg yolks
1 teaspoon grated orange rind
2 tablespoons orange juice
2 tablespoons sugar

Sift flour and ½ cup of the sugar to-
gether. Combine egg whites, salt, cream of tartar, and vanilla in large mixing bowl. Beat with rotary egg beater, flat wire whip, or at high speed of electric mixer until soft peaks form. Add remaining 1 cup of the sugar gradually, 4 tablespoons at a time, beating well after each addition. When beating by hand, beat 25 strokes or turns after each addition of sugar.

Sift flour mixture over egg whites, one-fourth at a time, and fold (do not stir or beat) in lightly. Turn bowl gradually and use 15 foldover strokes after each addition. After last addition use 10 to 20 extra strokes.

In another bowl, beat egg yolks, grated rind, juice, and 2 tablespoons sugar until very thick and light. Fold in ⅓ of the egg white mixture, using 15 strokes. Put batters into ungreased 10-inch tube pan, alternating yellow and white mixtures to give a marbled effect. Finish entire top with white batter. Bake in moderate oven (375°F.) 35 to 40 minutes, or until cake springs back when pressed lightly. Cool cake in pan, upside down, 1 to 2 hours. Then loosen from sides and center tube with knife and gently remove cake. Frost with Orange or Lemon Butter Cream Frosting (p. 57), or serve with fresh fruit and whipped cream.

## Fantasy Sponge Cake

*Feather-light, delicate, moist — all describe this cake. Serve it as a glamorous six-layer torte.*

6 egg whites (about ¾ cup)
1 teaspoon cream of tartar
1½ cups sifted sugar
1⅓ cups sifted Swans Down Cake Flour
½ teaspoon Calumet Baking Powder
½ teaspoon salt
6 egg yolks (about ½ cup)
¼ cup water
1 teaspoon lemon extract

Combine egg whites and cream of tartar in large bowl. Beat until soft mounds begin to form. (Beat at high speed of electric beater or use sturdy egg beater or wire whip.) Add ½ cup of the sugar gradually, 2 tablespoons at a time, and continue beating until very stiff peaks form. (Do not underbeat.)

Sift flour, baking powder, salt, and remaining 1 cup of the sugar into small bowl. Add egg yolks, water, and extract; beat with a spoon just until blended (about 75 strokes).

Fold egg yolk mixture into stiffly beaten egg whites, using about 30 fold-over strokes. (Do not stir or beat.)

Pour batter into ungreased 10-inch tube pan. Cut gently through batter to remove large air bubbles. Bake in moderate oven (375°F.) about 35 minutes, or until cake springs back when pressed lightly with finger. Remove from oven. Cool cake in pan, upside down, 1 to 2 hours. Then loosen from sides and center tube with knife and remove cake.

**Six Layer Torte.** Prepare Fantasy Sponge Cake as directed, pouring batter into three ungreased 8-inch layer pans. Bake in moderate oven (375°F.) about 15 minutes. Cool cakes upside down in pans about 1 hour. Split each layer horizontally. Spread Hungarian Chocolate Frosting (using 1½ times the recipe on p. 57) between layers, on top, and sides of cake.

## Cocoa Sponge Roll

*Sheer elegance when filled with pistachio cream and coated with chocolate.*

⅔ cup sifted Swans Down Cake Flour
¾ teaspoon Calumet Baking Powder
¼ teaspoon salt
⅓ cup Baker's Cocoa
1 cup plus 2 tablespoons sugar
6 eggs, unbeaten (at room temperature)
1½ teaspoons vanilla

Sift flour, baking powder, salt, cocoa, and ¼ cup of the sugar together. Beat eggs in large bowl until thick

and light in color. Add remaining sugar gradually, 1 tablespoon at a time, beating after each addition. Fold in flour mixture, one-third at a time. Blend in vanilla. Pour batter into a 15x10x1-inch pan which has been greased, lined on bottom with paper, and greased again. Bake in moderate oven (350°F.) 22 to 24 minutes, or until top springs back when pressed lightly with finger.

Cool cake in pan 3 to 5 minutes. Then turn immediately upside down on a clean towel, sprinkled with confectioners' sugar. Remove paper; trim off crusts. Roll up quickly, rolling the towel up with the cake to prevent the cake from sticking together. Cool on cake rack about 30 minutes. Then unroll carefully and remove cloth. Fill roll with desired filling and reroll.

**Pistachio Sponge Roll.** Spread cooled cake with Pistachio Whipped Cream (p. 61) and reroll. Spread ½ recipe of Hungarian Chocolate Frosting (p. 57) on rolled cake. Chill until serving time.

**Chocolate Tier Cake.** Cool Cocoa Sponge Roll upside down on sugared towel. *Do not roll up.* Then cut in four equal parts, making four layers. Spread 2 cups prepared Dream Whip or sweetened whipped cream, between layers. Then spread top and sides with Fluffy Chocolate Butter Frosting (p. 60). Chill until ready to serve.

## Old-Fashioned Cake Roll

*An old-fashioned cake traditionally filled with a tart, red jelly. Try some of the variations, too.*

¾ cup sifted Swans Down Cake Flour
¾ teaspoon Calumet Baking Powder
¼ teaspoon salt
4 eggs (at room temperature)
¾ cup sugar
1 teaspoon vanilla

Sift flour, baking powder, and salt together. Beat eggs in large bowl with sturdy egg beater or at high speed of electric mixer. Add sugar gradually and beat until mixture becomes fluffy, thick, and light-colored. Gradually fold in flour; then vanilla.

Pour batter into 15x10x1-inch pan which has been greased on bottom and sides, then lined on bottom with paper and greased again. Bake in hot oven (400°F.) 13 minutes.

Turn cake out onto cloth which has been sprinkled lightly with confectioners' sugar. Quickly remove paper and trim off crisp edges of cake. Then roll cake, rolling cloth up in cake, and place on rack to cool, about 30 minutes. Unroll and remove cloth. Spread with desired filling. Roll up again, leaving end of cake underneath. Sprinkle with additional confectioners' sugar or spread with a glaze.

**Jelly Roll.** Spread cooled cake with 1 cup tart red jelly. Roll up again, then sprinkle with confectioners' sugar.

**Jam Cake Roll.** Spread cooled cake with mixture of ¾ cup strawberry or cherry jam and ½ cup heavy cream, whipped. Roll up again and sprinkle with confectioners' sugar. Chill until ready to serve.

**Strawberry Cream Roll.** Spread cooled cake with sweetened whipped cream and top with thinly sliced fresh strawberries. Roll up again and sprinkle with confectioners' sugar. Chill until ready to serve. Serve with additional whipped cream and strawberries.

**Chocolate Roll.** Spread cooled cake with Chocolate Cream Filling (p. 61). Reroll and sprinkle with confectioners' sugar. Chill until ready to serve.

**Chocolate-Glazed Sponge Roll.** Spread cooled cake with prepared Dream Whip or whipped cream and reroll. Then spread with Sweet Chocolate Glaze (p. 60). Chill until ready to serve.

**Eight-Layered Sponge Cake.** Cool cake upside down on sugared towel. *Do not roll up.* Then cut into 4 equal pieces; split each piece to make 8 thin layers. Fill and frost with Fluffy Chocolate Butter Frosting (p. 60).

*An appetizing array — just a small sample of the delicious cakes that you can make when you start with a box of cake mix.*

SECTION 4

GENERAL FOODS KITCHENS

# The Mix-Made Cake

The biggest change in recent years on the American kitchen scene has been the growing popularity of convenience foods. One of the best-liked of these make-it-with-a-mix foods is the cake mix. Because of the numerous kinds and flavors of mixes available, you can make practically any cake, plain or fancy, in a minimum amount of time with a maximum amount of success.

When you bake a cake from a mix, first read through the recipe and follow the simple one-two-three label directions to the letter. These directions usually give a number of suitable pan sizes. Choose from among them according to your plans for the final cake. With many cake mixes you can often duplicate the made-from-scratch cake recipes in the previous chapters. But here are some suggestions for mix-made cakes with a plus — elegant additions that make these cakes your own exclusive creation.

*Party Nut Cake:* Prepare any Swans Down shortening cake mix as directed on package. Stir ¾ cup very finely chopped nuts and ¼ teaspoon salt into batter. Bake in two 9-inch layer pans as directed on package. Frost cooled cake with a fluffy or butter cream frosting and garnish with additional nuts.

**Mocha Spice Cake:** Prepare Swans Down Devil's Food Cake Mix according to package directions, beating ½ teaspoon cinnamon, ¼ teaspoon allspice, ¼ teaspoon nutmeg, and 4 teaspoons Instant Maxwell House Coffee into mix along with eggs and water. Bake as directed, using desired pan. Cool. Frost with a fluffy white frosting.

**Harvest Cake:** Prepare Swans Down Butterscotch Cake Mix as directed on package, *reducing water to 1 cup*. Add ½ cup sweetened applesauce, ½ teaspoon cinnamon, ¼ teaspoon nutmeg, and ½ cup chopped raisins to the mix along with eggs and water. Bake in two 9-inch layer pans as directed. Cool. Frost with Sea Foam Frosting (p. 56).

**Pineapple Upside-Down Cake:** Melt 1 cup firmly packed brown sugar with ⅓ cup butter over low heat; spread in 13x9x2-inch pan. Arrange 1¼ cups (1 lb. can) canned drained crushed pineapple (or 8 slices drained canned pineapple, cut in quarters) over sugar mixture. Sprinkle with 2 tablespoons pineapple juice and ½ cup chopped nuts. Prepare any Swans Down shortening cake mix as directed on package and pour carefully over fruit mixture in pan. Bake in moderate oven (350°F.) 55 to 60 minutes. Cool cake 5 minutes, then invert on serving plate. Let stand 1 minute before removing pan. Serve warm with prepared Dream Whip or sweetened whipped cream.

**Peanut Butter Cake:** Prepare Swans Down Sugar Maple Cake Mix as directed on package, adding ⅓ cup chunk-style peanut butter to mix along with eggs and water. Bake as directed in two 9-inch pans for 30 to 35 minutes. Frost cooled cake with prepared Dream Whip or sweetened whipped cream.

**Pumpkin Cake:** Prepare Swans Down Sugar Maple Cake Mix as directed on package, *reducing water to ¾ cup*. Add 1 cup canned pumpkin, ¾ teaspoon cinnamon, ¾ teaspoon mace, ¼ teaspoon ginger, and ¼ teaspoon

baking soda to mix along with eggs and water. Bake as directed in two 8-inch layer pans for 30 to 35 minutes. Cool. Frost with Amber Whipped Cream (use 1½ times the recipe on p. 60).

**Lemon-Peach Cake:** Prepare Swans Down Lemon Chip Angel Food Mix as directed on package. Cool as directed, then cut horizontally into 3 even layers. Whip 2 cups heavy cream until soft peaks form. Spread cream and 2 cups (17 oz. can) drained canned sliced peaches between layers and on top of cake. Chill until serving time.

**Graham Cracker Torte:** Prepare Swans Down Sugar Maple Cake Mix as directed on package, *increasing water to 1½ cups* and adding 1 cup finely crushed graham cracker crumbs to mix along with eggs and water. Fold ½ cup finely chopped nuts into batter. Bake as directed in two 9-inch layer pans for 30 to 35 minutes. Split cooled layers horizontally and spread Creamy Vanilla Filling (p. 61) between these thin layers. Sprinkle top of cake with confectioners' sugar. Chill until ready to serve.

**Fresh Apple Cake:** Prepare Swans Down Sugar Maple Cake Mix as directed on package, *reducing water to 1 cup*. Add 1 cup coarsely chopped apple and ½ teaspoon cinnamon to mix along with eggs and water. Stir ⅓ cup finely chopped pecans into batter. Bake as directed in two 9-inch layer pans. Cool. Frost with Fluffy Frosting recipe on package.

**Sour Cream Cake:** Prepare Swans Down Lemon Flake Cake Mix as directed on package, *reducing water to ⅔ cup*. Add 1 cup sour cream and ¼ teaspoon baking soda to mix along with eggs and water. Bake as directed for two 8-inch layers. Frost cooled cake with Fluffy Orange Frosting (p. 55).

**Pineapple Cream Cheese Torte:** Prepare Swans Down Lemon Flake Cake Mix as directed on package, *reducing water to 1 cup*. Add a 5 oz.

jar pineapple cream cheese to mix along with water and eggs. Bake as directed for two 8-inch layers. Split cooled cake layers horizontally and spread these thin layers with Creamy Vanilla Filling (p. 61). Top cake with prepared Dream Whip or whipped cream and slivered toasted almonds.

***Spicy Peach Cake:*** Prepare Swans Down Lemon Flake Cake Mix as directed on package, *reducing water to 1 cup*. Add 1 cup drained chopped canned peaches and ½ teaspoon cinnamon to mix with eggs and water. Bake as directed in two 8-inch layer pans. Cool. Frost with Lemon Fluff Frosting (p. 56).

*Swirl Party Nut Cake (p. 43) with Sea Foam Frosting (p. 56), then coat the sides with finely chopped nuts.*

*Flakes of fluffy coconut lend flavor and texture to both the cake and frosting in Dixie Coconut Cake (p. 47).*

**Baked Alaska:** Prepare any Swans Down shortening cake mix as directed on package, baking in a 13x9x2-inch pan. Cool. Beat 6 egg whites until foamy. Gradually add ¾ cup sugar, 2 tablespoons at a time, beating until meringue stands in stiff peaks. Place 2 quarts very firm brick ice cream on cake, forming a solid layer to within ½ inch of edge of cake. Cover all of cake and ice cream with meringue. Brown in hot oven (450°F.) about 5 minutes. Serves 20.

**Jam Cake:** Prepare any Swans Down shortening cake mix as directed on package, baking in two 8- or 9-inch layers. Cool. Spread about 1¼ cups jam or marmalade between layers and on top of cake.

**Marbled Mocha Spice Cake:** Prepare Swans Down White or Yellow Cake Mix as directed on package, adding ½ teaspoon vanilla to mix along with the eggs and water. To 1½ cups of the batter add a mixture of ½ teaspoon cinnamon, ¼ teaspoon cloves, 1 teaspoon Instant Maxwell House Coffee, and 1 tablespoon water; mix well. Grease and flour two 8-inch layer pans. Spoon plain and spice batters alternately into pans. Cut through batter with a knife to marble. Bake as directed on package. Cool. Frost with Fluffy Chocolate Butter Frosting (p. 60).

*Dixie Coconut Cake:* Prepare Swans Down White or Yellow Cake Mix as directed on package, adding ¾ cup Angel Flake Coconut. Bake as directed in two 8-inch layer pans. Frost cooled cake with Fluffy Seven Minute Frosting (p. 55) and sprinkle with additional Angel Flake Coconut.

*Chocolate Coconut Cake:* Prepare Swans Down White Cake Mix as directed on package, folding 2 squares Baker's Unsweetened Chocolate, coarsely grated, into the batter. Bake as directed in two 9-inch layer pans. Split cooled layers horizontally. Fold 1 cup Baker's Angel Flake Coconut into 4 cups (use 2 envelopes) prepared Dream Whip or 1½ cups heavy cream, whipped. Spread between the layers and on top of cake. Spread ½ recipe Hungarian Chocolate Frosting (p. 57) on sides of cake. Garnish top of cake with an additional ⅓ cup Baker's Coconut.

*Chocolate Peppermint Cake:* Prepare Swans Down Devil's Food Cake Mix as directed on package, adding ¼ teaspoon peppermint extract to mix along with eggs and water. Bake as directed on package using desired pan size. Cool. Frost with a fluffy white frosting.

*Sunshine Cake:* Prepare Swans Down Yellow Cake Mix as directed on package, adding 1 tablespoon grated orange or lemon rind to mix along with water and eggs. Bake as directed on package using desired pan size. Frost cooled cake with Orange or Lemon Butter Cream Frosting (p. 57).

*Sunshine Cupcakes:* Prepare Swans Down Yellow or White Cake Mix as above, baking batter in cupcake pans as directed on package. Cool. Frost with Orange or Lemon Butter Cream Frosting (p. 57).

*Cocoa Cream Cupcakes:* Prepare Swans Down Devil's Food Cake Mix as directed on package. Bake as directed for cupcakes. Cut off tops of cooled cupcakes and hollow out inside. Fill with Cocoa Whipped Cream (p. 60). Replace tops and frost with additional Cocoa Whipped Cream. Chill until ready to serve.

*Cinnamon Toasted Cupcakes:* Prepare Swans Down Yellow or White Cake Mix as directed on package, baking in cupcake pans. Sprinkle 2 to 2½ tablespoons cinnamon-sugar mixture over batter before baking. These are wonderful served warm.

*Slices of canned peaches and whipped cream make the filling and frosting in Lemon-Peach Cake (p. 44).*

*A spray of lilies of the valley lends a glamorous finishing touch to this de luxe, elegant Pistachio Sponge Roll (p. 40).*

SECTION 5

GENERAL FOODS
KITCHENS

# The Frosting on the Cake

A cake may be laden with virtues, light in texture, delicious in flavor, moist, and lovely to look at, but without frosting it seems less than perfect. A cake comes into its full glory only when decked out in a swirled, whirled coating of sweetness. Frostings have a very practical purpose, too. Frosted cakes stay moist and fresh-tasting much longer than unfrosted ones.

There are probably as many kinds of frostings as there are cakes to be frosted, deep rich and chocolate to snow-white and fluffy. Some are flecked with fragments of nuts and chocolate, others are thick with bits of fruits, but they are all designed to please the eye and the taste as well. Frostings generally fall into one of three categories.

*Fluffy cooked frostings:* Seven Minute and Sea Foam Frostings are excellent examples of this type of frosting. Sugar, egg whites, water, and flavorings are beaten over boiling water until the mixture stands in stiff peaks. A frosting of similar nature can be made by cooking a sugar-water syrup to a given temperature, then beating it slowly into whipped egg whites. Both of these frostings spread easily and will mound and swirl to perfection. Because they make a cake look so glamorous, these frostings are our favorite for photography. When fresh these frostings tend to be

49

sticky, thus are not ideal to transport (picnics and church suppers). They are best left uncovered the first couple of hours. If kept several days they may develop a thin sugary crust.

*Cooked fudge frostings:* These are actually soft fudges spread on cakes. A sugar mixture is cooked to a certain temperature (usually the soft ball stage), cooled, then beaten until creamy before spreading. This kind of frosting needs a good strong arm for beating (as does fudge) and it is not the easiest to work with because it sets quickly. If it should set before you've finished spreading it, place the pan over hot water and beat in a teaspoon or two of warm water or milk.

*Uncooked or butter cream frostings:* These frostings use confectioners' sugar — sugar that's been crushed and pulverized to a powdery fineness. The finer the sugar, the more moist the frosting will be and stay. The sugar is added in small amounts to a creamed butter or butter mixture, then beaten to a good spreading consistency. This is a consistency that is not so thin it runs off the cake, nor so thick that when it's spread it tears the cake. We frequently add whole eggs, egg whites, or yolks to frostings as part of the liquid for a creamier consistency.

*Filling and frosting cakes:* Always cool a cake thoroughly before frosting and brush away any loose crumbs from the sides. In our baking kitchen, we arrange strips of waxed paper around the edge of the plate before placing the first layer on the plate. These strips catch stray drips and frosting smears and pull out easily once the cake is completely frosted. Place the first layer, top side down, on the plate and spread frosting or filling completely to the edge. Allow the filling to set a few minutes, then place the second layer, bottom side down, on the filling.

Next frost the sides of both layers using upward strokes. Then pile the remaining frosting on top of the cake and spread to the edges to make

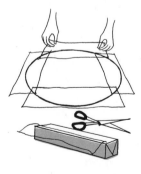

swirls and ripples with a spatula or the back of a spoon. For cakes you want to look especially nice, spread the sides with a thin layer or base coat of frosting first. This provides a smooth working surface upon which to spread more frosting.

In the following chart we have suggested ideal amounts of butter cream or fudge-type frosting for various sized cakes. More or less frosting may be used depending upon the tenderness of the cake and the ease with which the frosting spreads. In all cases, more (about twice as much) of the fluffy-type frostings, Seven Minute and Sea Foam, should be used.

| | Center | Sides | Top | Total |
|---|---|---|---|---|
| 8-inch layer cake | ½ cup | 1 cup | ¾ cup | 2¼ cups |
| 9-inch layer cake | ⅔ cup | 1¼ cups | ¾ cup | 2⅔ cups |
| 8-inch square | | ⅔ cup | ⅔ cup | 1⅓ cups |
| 9-inch square | | 1 cup | 1 cup | 2 cups |
| 13x9-inch cake | | 1 cup | 1⅓ cups | 2⅓ cups |
| 24 cupcakes | | | 2¼ cups | |
| 10-inch tube cake | | 1½ cups | ¾ cup | 2¼ cups |

Some tube cakes are placed top side down before frosting. When we want to keep sheet cakes (cakes baked in oblong pans) moist and fresh for a couple of days, we frost them right in the pan.

***Cutting the cake:*** The first requirement for well cut cakes is a thin, pointed, very sharp knife. Serrated (a saw-like edge) or scalloped-edge knives are particularly good for sponge-type cakes. They are excellent for yeast breads, too. Insert the point of the knife into the cake and, keeping the point angled down slightly, *saw* through the cake with a *gentle* back and forth motion. Put very little pressure on the knife, let the sharp edge do the work. When you're cutting six cakes at one time, as we so often do, there is always at least one with a frosting that sticks to the knife. We dip cake knives in hot water to take the "stick" out of frosting.

The wedge of a round cake and the slice from a square layer cake are familiar to almost everyone. To cut cakes to best advantage, especially large cakes for a crowd, try one of the ways diagramed below. Broken lines show first cuts to be made.

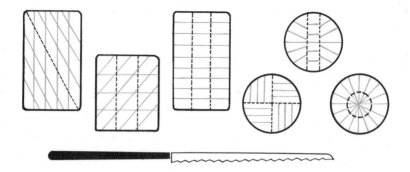

## CAKE DECORATING

Decorating cakes and cupcakes may be as simple or as complicated as you wish to make it. Here are some quick-and-easy suggestions for "prettying-up" your cakes.

### FESTIVE FROSTING TIPS AND TOPPERS:

*Tinted Frosting:* Add food coloring to frosting gradually — drop by drop. The amount of coloring is easier to control if it's poured from the tip of a spoon. Blend the coloring in thoroughly, scraping the sides of the bowl frequently so that frosting is evenly tinted.

*Toasted Coconut:* Spread coconut thinly on shallow baking pan. Bake in moderate oven (350°F.) 8 to 12 minutes, or until browned. Stir coconut or shake pan often to toast evenly.

*Tinted Coconut:* Dilute a few drops of food coloring in a small amount of water in a bowl. Add coconut and toss with a fork until coconut is evenly tinted. Or put coconut in a jar, filling it half way. Sprinkle diluted coloring over coconut, cover jar, and shake vigorously until evenly colored. (A teaspoon of diluted coloring is enough to tint about 1⅓ cups coconut.)

*Bittersweet Coating:* Melt 1 square Baker's Unsweetened Chocolate with 1 teaspoon butter or margarine in saucepan over hot water. Cool slightly, then pour from tip of spoon over frosting in desired pattern.

*Chocolate Curls:* Melt Baker's Dot Chocolate or Semi-Sweet Chocolate Chips over hot water. Pour in a thin layer on a lightly greased baking sheet or inverted cake or pie pan. Chill until firm. Then scrape chocolate with wide spatula to make large thin curls.

*Chocolate Lettering:* Melt Baker's Dot Chocolate or Semi-Sweet Chocolate Chips over hot water. Pour from the tip of a spoon on waxed paper in the form of letters or numerals. Chill until firm, then carefully peel paper away from chocolate. Stand letters or numerals upright on frosted cake.

### EASY CAKE DECORATING

*Snow Peak Cake:* Frost a cake generously with Fluffy Seven Minute (p. 55) or Snowy Boiled Frosting, (p. 56). Press flat side of spatula gently into frosting, then lift off. Frosting will follow spatula forming a peak. Repeat all over surface of frosting.

*Shadow Cake:* Frost cake with a white or pastel frosting. Pour Bittersweet Coating (p. 52) from the tip of a spoon over the top of the cake or along edges, letting it run down sides.

*Swirl Cake:* Pour Bittersweet Coating (p. 52) in continuous circles over top of a cake frosted with a fluffy cooked frosting. With a spatula, swirl chocolate into frosting.

*Dotted Swiss Cake:* Arrange Baker's Semi-Sweet Chocolate (Caramel or Lemon) Chips over the top and/or sides of a frosted cake. Press chips gently into frosting.

*Carousel Cake:* Mark off six equal wedges on a round layer cake which has been frosted in white. Pat Baker's Angel Flake Coconut, which has been tinted various colors, over wedges. See page 52 for tinting instructions.

*Patchwork Quilt Cake:* Mark a sheet cake into equal squares or diamonds. Use chopped nuts, chopped cherries, coconut (plain or tinted), pastel mint patties, and crushed candies to garnish the various squares or diamonds.

*Mint Marble Cake:* Place about 20 chocolate-covered peppermint patties over top of a freshly baked 9x9x2-inch cake. Return to oven 3 to 4 minutes. As soon as patties melt, take cake from oven and pull spatula back and forth through mints spreading them and giving a marbled effect.

*Black Magic Cake:* Sprinkle 1 cup (6 oz. package) Baker's Semi-Sweet Chocolate Chips over 9x9x2-inch cake as soon as it comes from the oven. Return to oven for 3 to 4 minutes to soften chips. Spread softened chips over cake. Sprinkle with chopped peanuts.

*Hill and Vale Cake:* Spread a cake with fluffy frosting. Then dip a spoon into melted chocolate and turn tip of spoon into frosting surface. Repeat here and there all over surface of cake.

*White Lace Cake:* Place a frilly lace doily on unfrosted cake. Sift confectioners' sugar over doily-topped cake, then carefully lift off doily.

*Chocolate Lace Cake:* Grate Baker's Dot or Unsweetened Chocolate, using a very fine grater. Place a paper doily lightly on a frosted cake and sprinkle grated chocolate over doily. Carefully remove the doily.

*Circus Cake:* Press animal crackers into sides and over top of frosted cake.

*Pink Drift Cake:* Frost cake generously with Fluffy Seven Minute (p. 55) or Snowy Boiled Frosting (p. 56). Make deep swirls in frosting. Sprinkle Strawberry or Cherry Jell-O, as it comes from the box, lightly over the frosting — hit only the high spots.

## DECORATING WITH A TUBE

No one is born with a natural skill in using a pastry tube — only practice makes perfect. So don't be discouraged if your first attempt doesn't quite live up to your professional standards, your second will be better. An inverted cake or pie pan makes a good surface upon which to practice.

Equally as important as the technique is the frosting used. It should be soft enough to force through a tube easily, yet stiff enough to hold its shape. The following recipe is particularly good for decorating:

*Decorating Frosting:* Cream ¼ cup shortening; (butter or margarine makes frosting yellow and affects color when tinting) add ¾ cup sifted confectioners' sugar gradually, beating after each addition. Add ½ teaspoon vanilla and a dash of salt. Add 1¼ cups sifted confectioners' sugar to shortening mixture alternately with about 3 tablespoons milk. (Use only enough milk so that frosting will go through tube smoothly but still hold its shape.) Beat after each addition until smooth, then continue beating until creamy.

Tint (see p. 52) if desired. Makes ¾ cup.

There are literally hundreds of different tips that actually make the design in the frosting. These tips fit into commercially made tubes or bags (made of metal, plastic, or cloth) or you can make a bag from paper as follows:

1. Cut a square (no less than an 8-inch square) of parchment or bond paper in half diagonally making 2 triangles (Fig. 1). Cut 1 triangle for each color of frosting you plan to use.

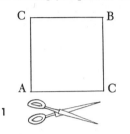

2. Following illustrations, bring corner A of triangle around to meet corner C (Fig. 2). Bring corner B around cone so that corners A and B are both meeting corner C. (Fig. 3).

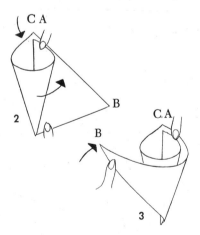

3. Fold point ABC down into cone (Fig. 4). Cut off ½ to ¾ inch from tip of cone (Fig 4). Drop desired tip into the cone.

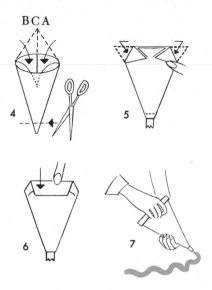

4. Half fill cone with frosting. Fold in top corners of cone, then fold top down (Figs. 5 and 6). Hold bag at top with right hand and press out frosting. Use left hand to guide tip (Fig. 7).

*Star Tip:* Of the hundreds of various shapes of tips used by bakers and professional cake decorators, the star tip is one of the most versatile — one of three basic tips needed for simple decorating. This tip makes rosettes (1, 2), letters (3), and borders (4).

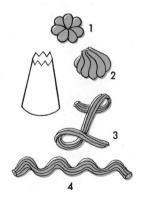

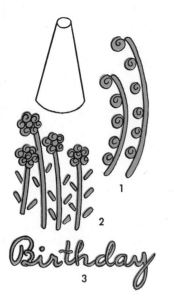

**Writing Tip:** This tip is used for stems and certain flowers such as lilies of the valley and forget-me-nots (1, 2). And as its name implies, it is used for writing and lettering (3).

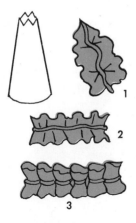

**Leaf tip:** This tip is used for leaves (1) and for borders. Use a steady pressure for plain borders (2) and an overlapping motion for frilled borders (3).

## Fluffy Seven Minute Frosting

*A fluffy light frosting with a high glossy sheen. It spreads easily into luscious looking swirls and whirls.*

2 egg whites, unbeaten
1½ cups sugar
Dash of salt
½ cup water
1 tablespoon light corn syrup
1¼ teaspoons vanilla

Combine egg whites, sugar, salt, water, and corn syrup in top of double boiler. Beat about 1 minute to mix thoroughly. Then place over boiling water and beat constantly with mixer or sturdy egg beater 7 minutes, or until frosting will stand in stiff peaks. (Stir frosting up from bottom of pan occasionally.)

Remove from boiling water. (For a very smooth and satiny frosting, pour in large bowl for final beating.) Add vanilla and beat 1 minute, or until thick enough to spread. Makes 5⅓ cups, or enough for tops and sides of two 8- or 9-inch layers, top and sides of a 13x9x-2-inch cake, or 2 dozen cupcakes.

*Fluffy Cherry Frosting.* Use recipe for Fluffy Seven Minute Frosting, adding 3 tablespoons maraschino cherry juice with the unbeaten egg white and substituting 1 teaspoon grated lemon rind for the vanilla.

*Coconut Marshmallow Frosting.* Use recipe for Fluffy Seven Minute Frosting. Fold in 1 cup marshmallows, quartered, before spreading on cake. Then sprinkle top and sides of cake with 1⅓ cups (about) Baker's Angel Flake Coconut while frosting is soft.

*Coffee Fluff Frosting.* Use recipe for Fluffy Seven Minute Frosting. Add 2 to 3 teaspoons Instant Maxwell House Coffee to egg white mixture before beating.

*Fluffy Orange Frosting.* Use recipe for Fluffy Seven Minute Frosting. Add 1 teaspoon orange extract and 2 teaspoons grated orange rind with vanilla.

**Fluffy Peppermint Frosting.** Use recipe for Fluffy Seven Minute Frosting, omitting the vanilla and adding ¼ teaspoon peppermint extract. Tint pale pink with red food coloring. Sprinkle frosting with crushed peppermint candy.

**Fluffy Chocolate Frosting.** Use recipe for Fluffy Seven Minute Frosting. Before spreading, *gently* stir in 2 squares Baker's Unsweetened Chocolate, which have been melted, then cooled.

**Lemon Fluff Frosting.** Use recipe for Fluffy Seven Minute Frosting, omitting vanilla. After final beating, fold in 2 tablespoons lemon juice.

**Pineapple Filling and Frosting.** Use recipe for Fluffy Seven Minute Frosting. Combine ½ cup of the frosting with ¾ cup drained canned crushed pineapple; spread between layers of cake. Then spread remaining frosting on top and sides of cake.

## Snowy Boiled Frosting

*Similar to old-fashioned divinity candy in flavor, texture, and consistency.*

2 cups sugar
1 cup water
Pinch of salt
1 teaspoon vinegar
2 egg whites
¾ teaspoon vanilla

Combine sugar, water, salt, and vinegar in a saucepan. Cook and stir over medium heat just until clear. Then cook without stirring until syrup spins a long thread when dropped from tip of spoon (or to a temperature of 240°F.).

Beat egg whites until soft peaks form. Add syrup in a very thin stream, beating constantly. After all syrup is added, continue beating until frosting will stand in stiff peaks. Mix in vanilla. Makes about 2¾ cups, or enough to frost top and sides of two 8- or 9-inch layers, or a 13x9x2-inch cake.

## Easy Chocolate Frosting

*A simple-to-make, easy-to-spread frosting with a deep chocolate flavor.*

3 to 4 squares Baker's Unsweetened Chocolate
3 tablespoons butter or margarine
4 cups sifted confectioners' sugar
⅛ teaspoon salt
7 tablespoons milk
1 teaspoon vanilla

Melt chocolate and butter over hot water. Combine sugar, salt, milk, and vanilla; blend. Add melted chocolate and butter and mix well. Let stand, stirring occasionally, until of right consistency to spread. If necessary, place bowl in pan of ice and water to hasten thickening. Makes 2 cups frosting, or enough to cover tops and sides of two 8- or 9-inch layers.

## Sea Foam Frosting

*A beige colored version of Seven Minute Frosting with a mellow brown-sugar flavor.*

2 egg whites, unbeaten
1½ cups firmly packed brown sugar
Dash of salt
⅓ cup water
1 teaspoon vanilla

Combine egg whites, sugar, salt, and water in top of double boiler. Beat with sturdy egg beater or electric beater 1 minute to mix thoroughly. Then place over boiling water and beat constantly with egg beater (or at high speed of electric mixer) 7 minutes, or until frosting will stand in stiff peaks. (Stir frosting up from bottom and sides of pan occasionally.) Remove from boiling water. Add vanilla and beat 1 minute, or until thick enough to spread. Makes 5¾ cups, or enough to cover tops and sides of two 9-inch layers (generously), three 8- or 9-inch layers, or about 2 dozen cupcakes.

*Sugarplum Frosting.* Use recipe for Sea Foam Frosting. Just before spreading fold in 1 cup cooked prunes, drained and cut in ½-inch pieces.

*Maple Sea Foam Frosting.* Prepare Sea Foam Frosting as directed, substituting ½ to ¾ teaspoon maple flavoring for the vanilla.

*Praline Frosting.* Prepare Sea Foam Frosting as directed. Just before spreading fold in ¾ cup chopped pecans.

## Butter Cream Frosting

*A smooth, creamy frosting that needs no cooking. Egg yolks lend a rich flavor and attractive yellow color.*

½ cup butter or margarine
⅛ teaspoon salt
1 pound (about 4 cups) sifted
   confectioners' sugar
2 egg yolks, unbeaten*
1 teaspoon vanilla
2 tablespoons milk (about)

* One whole egg may be substituted.

Cream butter until soft. Add salt and part of sugar gradually, blending after each addition. Then add egg yolks and vanilla; blend well. Add remaining sugar, alternately with milk, until of right consistency to spread, beating after each addition until smooth. Makes about 2½ cups, or enough to frost tops and sides of three 8-inch or two 9-inch layers, two 9x9x2-inch square cakes, one 13x9x2-inch cake, or the tops of 3 dozen cupcakes.

*Lemon Butter Cream Frosting.* Use recipe for Butter Cream Frosting, substituting 1 teaspoon grated lemon rind for the vanilla.

*Orange Butter Cream Frosting.* Use recipe for Butter Cream Frosting, substituting 1 teaspoon grated orange rind for the vanilla. If desired, orange juice may be used in place of the milk.

*Coffee Butter Cream Frosting.* Use recipe for Butter Cream Frosting, decreasing vanilla to ½ teaspoon and adding 1 tablespoon Instant Maxwell House Coffee along with 1 whole egg in place of the egg yolks.

*Chocolate Butter Cream Frosting.* Use recipe for Butter Cream Frosting, increasing milk to about 4 tablespoons and adding 3 or 4 squares Baker's Unsweetened Chocolate, melted, after first addition of sugar. Makes 2¾ cups.

## Hungarian Chocolate Frosting

*The red-chocolate color and high gloss of this frosting will lend eye appeal and glamour to any cake.*

4 to 5 squares Baker's Unsweetened
   Chocolate
2¼ cups sifted confectioners' sugar
¼ cup hot water
2 egg yolks or 1 whole egg, unbeaten
6 tablespoons soft butter or margarine

Melt chocolate; remove from heat and place in bowl. Add sugar and water, both at once; blend. Add egg yolks and beat thoroughly. Then add butter, a tablespoon at a time, beating thoroughly after each addition. Makes 2 cups plus 2 tablespoons frosting, or enough to cover top and sides of a 13x9x2-inch cake or two 8- or 9-inch layers.

*Note:* Divide all the ingredients in half to make about 1 cup of frosting, or enough to cover an 8- or 9-inch square cake or the outside of a cake roll.

## Quick Caramel Frosting

*A rich short-cut frosting with the texture and consistency of soft fudge.*

⅔ cup butter or margarine
1 cup firmly packed brown sugar
⅓ cup milk
3 cups sifted confectioners' sugar (about)

Melt butter in saucepan. Add brown sugar; cook over low heat 2 minutes, stirring constantly. Add milk and cook and stir until mixture comes to a boil. Remove from heat and cool about 10 minutes. Gradually add confectioners' sugar until frosting is of right consistency to spread, beating well after each addition. Makes 2 cups frosting, or enough to cover tops and sides of two 8- or 9-inch layers, or top and sides of a 9x9x2-inch cake.

**Quick White Fudge Frosting.** Prepare Quick Caramel Frosting as directed, using granulated sugar in place of brown sugar. Stir in 1 teaspoon vanilla before spreading.

## Chocolate Fudge Frosting

*For some this is the **only** chocolate frosting. It's a bit temperamental (not one of those easy-to-spread frostings) but well worth extra effort.*

3 cups sugar
3 tablespoons light corn syrup
1 cup milk
4 squares Baker's Unsweetened
  Chocolate
⅓ cup butter or margarine
1 teaspoon vanilla

Place the sugar, corn syrup, milk, and chocolate in a large saucepan. Cook over medium heat, stirring until sugar is dissolved. Continue cooking until mixture forms a very soft ball in cold water (or to temperature of 232° F.). Stir occasionally to prevent scorching.

Remove from heat, add butter without stirring, and cool until the bottom of the saucepan feels lukewarm (about 1 hour). Then add vanilla and beat until frosting is creamy and barely holds its shape. Spread quickly on cake before frosting hardens. Makes about 3 cups, or enough frosting for the tops and sides of two 8- or 9-inch layers.

*Note:* If frosting stiffens before spreading has been completed, add ½ to 1 teaspoon of water and beat until the frosting is smooth.

## Meringue Topping

*A moist, nut-topped meringue that bakes on the cake. Ideal for picnics.*

2 egg whites
Dash of salt
½ cup sugar
¼ teaspoon almond extract, optional
¼ cup chopped nuts

Beat egg whites and salt until foamy. Add sugar, 2 tablespoons at a time, beating well after each addition. Then continue beating until mixture stands in stiff peaks. Add flavoring and blend.

Spread lightly over cool cake in pan and sprinkle with nuts. Bake in hot oven (425°F.) 5 to 8 minutes, or until lightly browned. Makes enough topping for a 13x9x2-inch cake.

*Cupcakes become party fare when frosted and decorated with bits of candy, nuts, and fruit.*

*Brown Sugar Meringue Topping.* Prepare Meringue Topping, substituting firmly packed brown sugar for the granulated sugar. Omit almond extract.

## Coconut Pecan Frosting and Filling

*An out-of-the-ordinary, out-of-this-world frosting — rich in flavor and thick with coconut and pecans.*

1 cup evaporated milk
1 cup sugar
3 egg yolks
½ cup butter or margarine
1 teaspoon vanilla
1⅓ cups (about) Baker's Angel
   Flake Coconut
1 cup chopped pecans

Combine milk, sugar, egg yolks, butter, and vanilla in a saucepan. Cook over medium heat, stirring constantly, until thickened, about 12 minutes. Remove from heat. Add coconut and pecans. Beat until cool and of spreading consistency. Makes 2⅔ cups, or enough for tops of three 8- or 9-inch layers.

## Coconut Cream Cheese Frosting

*A superb flavor blend of browned butter and toasted coconut in a luscious, not too sweet cream cheese frosting.*

2 tablespoons butter or margarine
1⅓ cups (about) Baker's Angel
   Flake Coconut
⅓ cup butter or margarine
2 packages (3 oz. each) cream cheese
1 pound (about 4 cups) sifted
   confectioners' sugar
1 tablespoon milk (about)
½ teaspoon vanilla

Melt 2 tablespoons butter in saucepan. Add coconut, sauté until golden brown, stirring constantly. Remove from heat.
   Cream ⅓ cup butter, add cheese and blend. Add small amounts of sugar and milk alternately, beating after each addition. Add vanilla and ¾ cup of the coconut. Spread on cake. Sprinkle with remaining coconut. Makes 2¾ cups, or enough frosting to cover tops and sides of two 8- or 9-inch layers.

## Chocolate Cream Cheese Frosting

*Save this for Sunday-best cakes. It's expensive but worth every cent.*

2 packages (¼ pound each) Baker's
   German's Sweet Chocolate
2 packages (3 oz. each) cream cheese
2 tablespoons light cream
2 cups sifted confectioners' sugar
¼ teaspoon salt
1 teaspoon vanilla

Place chocolate in small bowl and set over hot water until melted. Cool slightly. Add cream cheese and cream; blend. Add sugar gradually, mixing well. Then add salt and vanilla. Makes 2 cups or enough to spread on tops and sides of two 8- or 9-inch layers, or the tops of about 30 cupcakes.

*Note:* Divide all ingredients in half, except salt, to make about 1 cup frosting, or enough to cover top of an 8- or 9-inch square cake.

## Fluffy Butter Frosting

*A happy combination of a butter cream and fluffy frosting. Both versions, vanilla and chocolate, are luscious.*

6 tablespoons butter or margarine
¼ teaspoon salt
1 teaspoon vanilla
1 pound (about 4 cups) sifted
   confectioners' sugar
2 egg whites, unbeaten
1 tablespoon milk (about)

Cream butter, salt, and vanilla together. Add sugar alternately with egg whites, beating well after each addition. Add milk and beat until smooth and of spreading consistency. Makes 2¼ cups frosting, or enough to cover tops and sides of two 8- or 9-inch layers.

**Fluffy Chocolate Butter Frosting.** Use recipe for Fluffy Butter Frosting, adding 3 squares Baker's Unsweetened Chocolate, melted, to the sugar-egg white mixture. Beat well. Increase milk to 2 or 3 tablespoons; add to chocolate mixture, and beat until frosting is of spreading consistency. Makes 2½ cups, or enough to frost tops and sides of two 8- (generously) or 9-inch layers.

## Orange Butter Glaze

*A smooth, shiny glaze with a nippy orange (or lemon) flavor.*

1½ tablespoons milk
1 tablespoon butter
1¼ cups sifted confectioners' sugar
1 tablespoon orange juice
½ teaspoon grated orange rind, optional

Heat milk and butter together. Stir in sugar and mix well. Add orange juice and rind; beat until smooth. Spread over cooled cake. Makes ½ cup, or enough to glaze top of 10-inch tube cake, an 8- or 9-inch square cake, or a 9x5x3-inch loaf.

**Lemon Butter Glaze.** Prepare Orange Butter Glaze, substituting lemon juice and rind for the orange juice and rind.

## Sweet Chocolate Glaze

*A thin, pourable chocolate glaze that lends a high gloss to cakes.*

1 package (¼ pound) Baker's German's Sweet Chocolate
1 tablespoon butter
3 tablespoons water
1 cup sifted confectioners' sugar
Dash of salt
½ teaspoon vanilla

Melt chocolate and butter in water over low heat. Combine sugar and salt in medium-size bowl. Add chocolate mixture gradually, blending well. Add vanilla. Makes ¾ cup glaze, or enough

to glaze top of 10-inch tube cake or an 8- or 9-inch square cake.

## German's Chocolate Filling

*Sweet, mild chocolate provides a marvelous flavor in this creamy filling.*

¼ cup milk
¼ cup granulated sugar
1 egg
1 package (¼ pound) Baker's German's Sweet Chocolate, broken into pieces
⅓ cup butter or margarine, softened
2½ cups sifted confectioners' sugar
1 teaspoon vanilla
1 cup finely chopped pecans

Combine milk, granulated sugar, and egg in a saucepan. Mix well. Cook and stir over low heat until mixture is thick. Remove from heat. Add chocolate and butter. Stir until chocolate is melted. Then beat until smooth and creamy. Blend in confectioners' sugar and vanilla. Add pecans. Mix well. (If filling becomes too thick, mix in a little milk.) Makes 2⅓ cups, or enough for tops of three 9- or four 8-inch cake layers.

## Whipped Cream Topping

*There's a secret to whipping cream — beat it only until it's thick and glossy.*

1 cup whipping cream
2 teaspoons sugar, optional
½ teaspoon vanilla, optional

Place cream, sugar, and vanilla in chilled bowl. Beat until cream holds its shape. (Do not overbeat.) Makes 2 cups.

**Cocoa Whipped Cream.** Use recipe for Whipped Cream Topping, increasing sugar to 2 tablespoons. Mix 2 tablespoons Baker's Cocoa and dash of salt with the sugar, add to cream, and chill 1 hour before beating.

**Amber Whipped Cream.** Use recipe for Whipped Cream Topping. Substitute ⅔ cup firmly packed brown sugar for granulated sugar. Chill sugar-cream mixture 1 hour before beating.

*Pistachio Whipped Cream.* Use recipe for Whipped Cream Topping, increasing cream to 1¼ cups, sugar to 2 tablespoons, vanilla to 1 teaspoon, and adding ½ teaspoon almond extract. Tint with 8 drops green coloring and 4 drops yellow coloring before beating.

*Coffee Whipped Cream.* Use recipe for Whipped Cream Topping, increasing sugar to 2 tablespoons and adding 1 to 2 teaspoons Instant Maxwell House Coffee to the cream before beating.

## Lemon Cake Filling

*The tart sweetness of this filling will lend a flavor lift to any cake.*

¾ cup sugar
3 tablespoons flour
1 egg yolk, slightly beaten
1 whole egg, slightly beaten
2 teaspoons butter or margarine
½ cup water
3 tablespoons lemon juice
¾ teaspoon grated lemon rind

Combine all ingredients except lemon rind in saucepan; mix thoroughly. Cook over medium heat, stirring constantly until mixture comes to a full boil and is thickened — about 5 minutes. Remove from heat, add grated lemon rind, and blend well. Cool. Makes 1¼ cups filling, or enough to spread between two 8- or 9-inch cake layers.

## Fluffy Whipped Topping

*A light fluffy topping with an unlimited number of variations.*

½ cup cold milk
½ teaspoon vanilla
1 envelope Dream Whip

Combine ingredients in a small bowl. Blend, then beat vigorously until soft peaks form. Cover and chill well before serving. Makes about 2 cups.

*Cocoa Fluff Topping.* Prepare Fluffy Whipped Topping, adding 2 tablespoons Baker's Cocoa and 2 tablespoons sugar to Dream Whip along with the milk. Makes 2¼ cups.

*Peppermint Topping.* Prepare Fluffy Whipped Topping as directed. Fold in ¼ cup crushed peppermint candy or a few drops peppermint extract. Makes about 2¼ cups.

*Fruited Whip Topping.* Prepare Fluffy Whipped Topping as directed. Fold in ¼ cup drained, diced, or crushed fruit such as pineapple or strawberries. Makes about 2¼ cups.

## Quick Cake Fillers

*Chocolate Cream Filling:* Prepare 1 package Jell-O Chocolate (Chocolate Mint, Vanilla, Butterscotch, or Coconut Cream) Pudding and Pie Filling as directed on package, using only 1½ cups milk. Then chill, stirring occasionally. Whip ½ cup heavy cream until thick and glossy. Fold into pudding. Makes about 2⅓ cups.

*Creamy Vanilla Filling:* Prepare 1 package Jell-O Vanilla (Chocolate, Chocolate Mint, Butterscotch, or Coconut Cream) Pudding and Pie Filling as directed on package, using only 1¾ cups milk. Then cool, stirring occasionally. Makes 1¾ cups.

*Quick Lemon Filling:* Prepare 1 package Jell-O Lemon Pudding and Pie Filling as package directs, using 1 whole egg in place of 2 egg yolks. Cool, stirring occasionally. Makes 2⅓ cups.

## Glossy Confectioners' Sugar Glaze

*A glossy, opaque white glaze that lends a finishing touch to cakes and sweet rolls.*

1 tablespoon hot milk (about)
1 cup sifted confectioners' sugar

Add milk gradually to sugar in small bowl. Blend until mixture is thin enough to spread over cake. Makes ⅓ cup.

*Cookies of all sizes and shapes, decorated with bright bits of candy and fruit, make a festive, delicious assortment for holidays and for everyday snacks.*

GENERAL FOODS
KITCHENS

# Cookies –
# From Bars to Stars

Whoever invented the cooky (we're willing to bet it was a grand-mother) must have been a good friend of some hungry children. Cookies are wonderful out-of-hand food for children (children of all ages). There is a treasure trove of cooky recipes on the following pages, most of them quick and easy to make. You'll have only one problem with them; they have no lasting qualities, they'll disappear as quickly as you put them into the cooky jar.

It is difficult to say what the perfect cooky should taste and look like — there are so many kinds. Some are soft and cake-like, some are rich and crisp, still others are almost brittle. Generally cookies fall into the follow-ing categories.

***Bars:*** These cookies have a rich, cake-like texture. They are exceed-ingly easy to make; they store and ship well. They are baked in square or rectangular pans, cooled, then cut in bars or squares. Brownies are prob-ably the best known bar cookies.

*Refrigerator:* These are usually round thin cookies with a crisp texture. The rather soft cooky dough is shaped into long rolls, wrapped in waxed paper or aluminum foil, and chilled for at least two hours. These rolls are then cut into thin crosswise slices (use a very sharp knife) and baked on a cooky sheet. The rolls of dough will keep for a week or so in the refrigerator (even longer in the freezer), so you can slice and bake the cookies as you need them.

*Drop:* Drop cookies can be soft with a cake-like texture, crisp, or even brittle. The characteristic common to all of them is a soft dough that is dropped in mounds on a cooky sheet and baked. As a result, they all have a more or less irregular shape.

*Shaped:* The dough for these cookies is fairly stiff or it's chilled until it is stiff enough to handle. Then it is molded by hand or cooky press into the desired shape — balls, wreaths, crescents, oblongs, or stars.

*Rolled:* These cookies are cut into various shapes from a rather stiff dough — stiff enough to be rolled a quarter to one-eighth inch thick. Because of the variety of shapes, these cookies can be quite decorative.

The baking sheet used for cookies should be kept shiny for even browning. Never use a sheet that is so large it touches the walls of the oven. Most cookies should be placed on racks to cool. Don't overlap or stack cookies before they are thoroughly cooled.

## Brownies

*Whatever can be said about Brownies has already been said hundreds of times — these are among the best.*

¾ cup sifted Swans Down Cake Flour
½ teaspoon Calumet Baking Powder
¼ teaspoon salt
⅓ cup shortening
2 or 3 squares Baker's Unsweetened
    Chocolate
2 eggs
1 cup sugar
½ cup chopped walnuts
1 teaspoon vanilla

Sift flour, baking powder, and salt together. Melt shortening and chocolate together over hot water. Beat eggs well, add sugar gradually, and beat thoroughly. Then add chocolate mixture and blend. Add flour and mix well; then stir in nuts and vanilla.

Bake in greased 8x8x2-inch pan in moderate oven (350°F.) 25 minutes for moist chewy Brownies, or 30 minutes for cake-like Brownies. Cool in pan; then cut in squares or rectangles. Makes about 20 Brownies.

*Nut-Glazed Brownies.* Use recipe for Brownies. Bake in moderate oven (350°F.) 20 minutes. Remove from oven and sprinkle ½ cup Baker's Semi-Sweet Chocolate Chips over top. Return to oven and bake 5 minutes longer, or until done. Immediately after removing from oven, spread the softened chocolate chips smoothly over top. Sprinkle with 2 tablespoons finely chopped nuts.

*Chocolate Chip Brownies.* Use recipe for Brownies. Spread batter in pan, sprinkle with ½ cup Baker's Semi-Sweet Chocolate Chips, then bake.

**Marshmallow Sundae Brownies.** Use recipe for Brownies. Spread batter in greased 13x9x2-inch pan. Bake in moderate oven (350°F.) 17 minutes, or until done. Immediately cover top with 24 marshmallows, cut in quarters. Cool. Then melt 1 cup (6-oz. package) Baker's Semi-Sweet Chocolate Chips over hot water; pour over marshmallows. Cool and cut in 2-inch squares. Makes 24 Brownies.

**Peppermint Brownies.** Use recipe for Brownies. Remove from oven; place 15 to 20 chocolate peppermint patties on top, and return to oven about 3 minutes to soften patties. Then, with a spatula, spread patties over top of Brownies.

## Scotch Bars

*A kissin' cousin to Brownies with a butterscotch flavor and a top well peppered with Baker's chips.*

1 cup sifted flour
½ teaspoon Calumet Baking Powder
⅛ teaspoon baking soda
½ teaspoon salt
½ cup chopped nuts
⅓ cup shortening
1 cup firmly packed brown sugar
1 tablespoon hot water
1 egg, slightly beaten
1 teaspoon vanilla
½ cup Baker's Semi-Sweet Chocolate, Lemon, or Caramel Chips

Sift flour, baking powder, soda, and salt together Add nuts and mix well. Melt shortening in saucepan; remove from heat. Add sugar and water; mix well. Cool slightly. Add egg and vanilla and blend. Then add flour mixture, a small amount at a time, mixing well after each addition. Turn into greased 9x9x2-inch pan. Sprinkle chips over top. Bake in moderate oven (350°F.) 20 to 25 minutes. (Do not overbake.) Cool in pan. Then cut into bars. Makes about 2 dozen bars.

## De Luxe Fudgy Brownies

*If any cooky out-Brownies Brownies, this is it! These are superbly rich, moist, and altogether wonderful.*

4 squares Baker's Unsweetened Chocolate
½ cup butter or margarine
4 eggs
2 cups sugar
1 cup sifted flour
1 teaspoon vanilla
1 cup coarsely chopped walnuts

Melt chocolate and butter together over hot water. Cool slightly. Beat eggs until foamy; gradually add sugar, beating thoroughly after each addition. Add chocolate mixture and blend. Stir in flour. Then add vanilla and nuts. Spread in greased 9x9x2-inch pan. Bake in moderate oven (325°F.) about 40 minutes. Cool in pan, then cut into squares or bars. Makes about 2 dozen Brownies.

## Apricot Bars

*A tart, tangy apricot filling lends a piquant flavor to these crunchy bars.*

1 cup chopped dried apricots
1 cup water
1¼ cups sifted Swans Down Cake Flour
½ teaspoon Calumet Baking Powder
⅛ teaspoon cinnamon
¼ cup Post Grape-Nuts Flakes, crushed
¼ cup butter or margarine
¾ cup firmly packed brown sugar
½ cup Baker's Angel Flake Coconut

Simmer apricots in water until liquid is absorbed, about 8 minutes. Cool. Sift flour, baking powder, and cinnamon together. Mix in crushed cereal. Cream butter and sugar together. Cut in dry ingredients to form a uniform crumb mixture. Mix in coconut.

Press about two-thirds of the crumb mixture firmly into an ungreased 8x8x2-inch pan. Spread the apricot mixture evenly over crumbs. Sprinkle with remaining crumb mixture. Bake in moderate oven (375°F.) for 20 to 25 minutes, or until golden brown. Cut in bars or squares. Serve warm with whipped cream or cool and serve as cookies. Makes 24 bars or 16 squares.

## Quick Coconut Macaroons

*A moist, chewy coconut cooky that's very easy to make.*

2 cups (7-oz. package) Baker's
   Fine-Grated Coconut
¾ cup sweetened condensed milk
Dash of salt
1 teaspoon vanilla
¼ teaspoon almond extract

Combine all ingredients and mix well. Drop by teaspoonfuls, 1 inch apart, on greased baking sheets. Bake in moderate oven (325°F.) about 15 minutes, or until golden brown. Remove from baking sheet at once. Makes 2½ dozen.

*Chocolate-Almond Macaroons.* Use recipe for Quick Coconut Macaroons. Add 1½ squares Baker's Unsweetened Chocolate, melted, ½ cup chopped almonds, and an additional 2 tablespoons condensed milk. Increase almond extract to ½ teaspoon.

*Chocolate-Fleck Macaroons.* Use recipe for Quick Coconut Macaroons, reducing coconut to 1½ cups, and adding 1 cup (6 oz. package) Baker's Semi-Sweet Chocolate Chips before mixing the ingredients.

*Cocoa Macaroons.* Use recipe for Quick Coconut Macaroons, omitting the almond extract. Add 3 tablespoons Baker's Cocoa with an additional 2 tablespoons condensed milk before mixing ingredients.

*Peanut Butter Macaroons.* Use recipe for Quick Coconut Macaroons, omitting the almond extract. Add ⅓ cup peanut butter with an additional 2 tablespoons condensed milk before mixing ingredients.

## Coconut Dream Squares

*A rich, buttery crust plus a coconut-nut topping equal a moist, chewy cooky that's a bit unusual.*

1¼ cups sifted Swans Down Cake Flour
1¼ cups firmly packed brown sugar
⅓ cup butter or margarine
2 eggs, unbeaten
½ teaspoon Calumet Baking Powder
1 teaspoon vanilla
1⅓ cups (about) Baker's Angel
   Flake Coconut
1 cup chopped walnuts

Combine 1 cup of the flour and ¼ cup of the sugar. Add butter; mix until thoroughly blended and smooth. Press in ungreased 9x9x2-inch pan; bake in moderate oven (350°F.) 15 minutes.

Meanwhile, beat eggs until light. Add remaining 1 cup sugar gradually, beating constantly until mixture is light and fluffy. Sift remaining ¼ cup flour and the baking powder together and fold into egg mixture. Add vanilla, coconut, and nuts and mix thoroughly. Spread on top of baked mixture in pan and return to oven. Bake 20 to 25 minutes longer, or until lightly browned. Cut in squares while warm. Makes about 2 dozen squares.

## Meringue Crunch Bars

*These are good "keepers" — even better the day after they are made.*

1 cup Post Grape-Nuts
3 egg whites
¾ cup firmly packed brown sugar
1 teaspoon Calumet Baking Powder
¼ teaspoon salt
½ cup chopped pecans
1 teaspoon vanilla

Place cereal, about one-fourth cup at a time, on board, or on board between waxed paper. Crush with rolling pin until cereal resembles coarse meal.

Beat egg whites until foamy through-

66

out. Add sugar gradually, beating well after each addition. Then continue beating until stiff peaks form. Fold in cereal and remaining ingredients.

Bake in greased 8x8x2-inch pan in slow oven (325°F.) 25 to 30 minutes, or until lightly browned. While still warm, cut into bars or squares. Remove from pan and cool on racks. Makes about 20 bars.

## Chocolate Pecan Drops

*Tender, rich chocolate cookies topped with a shiny glaze and pecans.*

1⅔ cups sifted Swans Down Cake Flour
½ teaspoon salt
½ teaspoon baking soda
½ cup shortening
1 cup firmly packed brown sugar
1 egg, well beaten
1 teaspoon vanilla
2 squares Baker's Unsweetened
    Chocolate, melted
½ cup milk
½ cup chopped pecans
1 cup pecan halves (about)

Sift flour, salt, and soda together. Cream shortening and sugar together until light and fluffy. Add egg, vanilla, and chocolate; blend well. Add dry ingredients alternately with milk, stirring well after each addition. Stir in chopped nuts. Drop by heaping teaspoonfuls, 2 inches apart, on greased baking sheets. Bake in moderate oven (350°F.) 10 to 12 minutes. Spread warm cookies with Mocha Chocolate Glaze. Top each cooky with a pecan half. Makes about 3 dozen cookies.

*Mocha Chocolate Glaze.* Combine 3 tablespoons Baker's Instant and 1 teaspoon Instant Maxwell House Coffee. Blend in 3 tablespoons hot water, 2 tablespoons butter or margarine, and ½ teaspoon vanilla. Gradually add 1½ cups sifted confectioners' sugar, beating after each addition. Beat until glaze

is of a good spreading consistency. Makes enough to frost 3 dozen cookies.

## Short-Cut Cookies

*Cookies from a cake mix — quick and easy, crisp and delicious.*

1 package Swans Down Cake Mix
    (any flavor)
½ cup soft shortening
1 tablespoon water
2 eggs, unbeaten

Empty half of cake mix into bowl. Add remaining ingredients and blend well. Then add the rest of the mix and beat until blended.

Drop by teaspoonfuls onto greased baking sheets. Bake in moderate oven (375°F.) 10 to 12 minutes. Store in airtight container. Makes about 4 dozen. *Note:* If desired, add 1 teaspoon vanilla when using Devil's Food, Yellow, or Chocolate Chip Cake Mix.

*Coconut Dream Squares (p. 66) and Melting Moments (p. 70) decorated with pecans are perfect tea-time snacks.*

## Raisin Jumbo Cookies

*No dainty delicacy these — they are hearty, man-sized cookies with an excellent spice-raisin flavor.*

2 cups raisins
1 cup water
4 cups sifted flour
1 teaspoon Calumet Baking Powder
1 teaspoon baking soda
1 teaspoon salt
½ teaspoon cinnamon
½ teaspoon nutmeg
1 cup shortening
1¾ cups sugar
2 eggs, slightly beaten
1 teaspoon vanilla
½ cup chopped nuts

Bring raisins and water to a boil. Boil until the raisins are plump — about 3 minutes. Cool. Sift flour, baking powder, soda, salt, and spices together.

Cream shortening and sugar together until light and fluffy. Add eggs and vanilla and mix well. Stir in the raisins and any remaining water. Gradually add the flour mixture, blending thoroughly after each addition. Stir in nuts.

Drop by tablespoonfuls about 1 inch apart on greased baking sheets. Bake in a moderate oven (375°F.) 12 to 15 minutes. Makes about 3½ dozen.

## Medallion Sugar Cookies

*A crisp, old-fashioned sugar cooky with a colorful sugar topping. Cut tiny stars and rounds from rolled dough "scraps" to save rerolling.*

3⅔ cups sifted Swans Down Cake Flour
2½ teaspoons Calumet Baking Powder
½ teaspoon salt
⅔ cup shortening
1½ cups sugar
2 eggs, unbeaten
1 teaspoon vanilla
4 teaspoons milk

Sift flour, baking powder, and salt together. Cream shortening; add sugar gradually, creaming well. Add eggs, one at a time, beating thoroughly after each. Add vanilla. Add flour, alternately with milk, mixing well after each addition. Chill 3 to 4 hours, or overnight. Roll out very thin (less than ⅛ inch thick) on lightly floured surface. Cut with floured 3-inch scalloped cutter and sprinkle with white or colored sugar. Bake on ungreased sheets in hot oven (400°F.) for 9 minutes, or until done. Makes 6 dozen cookies.

*Note:* If desired, cookies may be decorated with Jell-O Gelatin instead of sugar. While still warm, brush cookies lightly with slightly beaten egg white, honey, or light corn syrup. Sprinkle with Jell-O Gelatin (any flavor).

## Molasses Drop Cookies

*If you've a hankering for grandmother's old-fashioned molasses cookies, try these.*

3 cups sifted Swans Down Cake Flour
1½ teaspoons baking soda
½ teaspoon salt
1 teaspoon ginger
1½ teaspoons cinnamon
½ cup shortening
1 cup sugar
1 egg, unbeaten
½ cup molasses
1 cup buttermilk
½ teaspoon vanilla

Sift flour, soda, salt, and spices together. Cream shortening; add sugar gradually, creaming until light and fluffy. Add egg and beat well; then stir in molasses. Add flour alternately with buttermilk, mixing well after each addition. Stir in vanilla. Chill until firm enough to hold shape — 1 to 2 hours. Drop from teaspoon on lightly greased baking sheets, placing about 2 inches apart. Bake in hot oven (400°F.) 8 to 10 minutes, or until done. Slide off baking sheet with a spatula. Makes 6 dozen cookies.

*Note:* Chill cooky dough between bakings, if necessary.

**Molasses Raisin Cookies.** Use recipe for Molasses Drop Cookies, adding 1 cup raisins to the dough.

**Molasses-Chip Cookies.** Use recipe for Molasses Drop Cookies, adding 1 cup (6-oz. package) Baker's Semi-Sweet Chocolate Chips to the dough.

### Chewy Coconutty Chocolate Cookies

*A moist, chewy macaroon with a strong chocolate flavor laced with peanut butter.*

3 squares Baker's Dot Chocolate, melted
¼ cup peanut butter
1 cup sweetened condensed milk
¼ teaspoon salt
1 teaspoon vanilla
1⅓ cups (about) Baker's Angel
    Flake Coconut

Combine melted chocolate and peanut butter; stir until smooth. Add milk, salt, vanilla, and coconut. Stir until all ingredients are blended. Drop from teaspoon on well-greased baking sheets. Bake in a moderate oven (350°F.) 10 to 12 minutes. Remove from baking sheet while still warm. Makes 3 dozen.

*These Scotch Bars (p. 65) feature a polka dot topping of chocolate chips.*

### Beacon Hill Cookies

*This crisp little meringue cooky can be made with chocolate or lemon chips — both are equally good.*

2 egg whites
⅛ teaspoon salt
½ cup sugar
½ teaspoon vinegar
½ teaspoon vanilla
½ cup Baker's Angel Flake Coconut
¼ cup chopped walnuts
1 cup (6-oz. package) Baker's Semi-Sweet Chocolate or Lemon Chips, melted

Beat egg whites and salt until foamy throughout. Add sugar very gradually, beating well after each addition. Then continue beating until stiff peaks form. Add vinegar and vanilla and beat well. (Entire beating process takes about 10 minutes.) Fold in coconut, nuts, and the melted chips.

Drop from teaspoon onto greased baking sheets. Bake in moderate oven (350°F.) 10 minutes. Makes 2½ to 3 dozen cookies.

### Maple Lace Wafers

*A crisp, lacy-thin cooky to be served plain or rolled and filled.*

½ cup Log Cabin Syrup
¼ cup butter or margarine
½ cup sifted flour
¼ teaspoon salt

Combine syrup and butter in saucepan. Place over high heat, bring to a boil, and boil hard ½ minute. Remove from heat. Sift flour and salt together. Add to hot syrup all at once, blending thoroughly. Drop from teaspoon, about 3 inches apart, onto greased baking sheets. Bake in moderate oven (350°F.) for 8 to 9 minutes.

Remove from oven and allow to cool about 1 minute. Then remove each wafer. If desired, quickly roll up in

69

tube shape. Place on rack to cool. If wafers harden before they can be rolled, return to oven for a few seconds. Store in airtight container. Serve plain or filled with Fruited Whip Topping or Coffee Whipped Cream (p. 61). Makes 2 dozen wafers.

**Spicy Lace Wafers.** Use above recipe, adding ¾ teaspoon cinnamon, ½ teaspoon ginger, and ½ teaspoon cloves to the flour before sifting with the salt.

## Melting Moments

*A rich cooky that's not too sweet — makes a pleasant, interesting contrast in a cooky assortment.*

½ cup cornstarch
1½ cups sifted confectioners' sugar
3 cups sifted flour
2 cups (1 pound) softened
   butter or margarine
1½ teaspoons vanilla
4 cups (about) Baker's Angel
   Flake Coconut

Sift cornstarch, sugar, and flour together. Blend butter and vanilla into dry ingredients until a soft dough is formed. Chill if desired, then shape into small balls, about ½ inch in diameter. Roll in coconut and place about 1 inch apart on ungreased baking sheets. Bake in slow oven (300°F.) 20 to 25 minutes, or until coconut is golden brown. Makes 9 dozen cookies.

## Coconut Butter Cookies

*A buttery old-country cooky intricately shaped with a cooky press.*

1 cup butter or margarine
⅔ cup firmly packed light brown sugar
2 egg yolks
2 teaspoons vanilla
2¼ cups sifted flour
¼ teaspoon salt
2 egg whites
2 teaspoons water
Baker's Angel Flake Coconut, tinted

Cream butter and sugar together until light and fluffy. Mix in egg yolks and vanilla. Add flour and salt; mix well. Mold dough with a cooky press into desired shapes on ungreased baking sheets. Bake in hot oven (400°F.) 8 to

*Top Medallion Sugar Cookies (p. 68) with plain or colored sugar, nuts, and fruits for a decorative assortment.*

10 minutes. Remove and cool on rack. Combine egg whites with water and brush over cooled cookies. Sprinkle with coconut. Makes about 3 dozen.

## Coconut Oatmeal Cookies

*A happy combination of an oatmeal cooky and a coconut macaroon.*

1 cup sifted flour
½ teaspoon Calumet Baking Powder
½ teaspoon salt
½ teaspoon baking soda
⅓ cup shortening
½ cup granulated sugar
½ cup firmly packed brown sugar
1 egg, unbeaten
1 teaspoon vanilla
½ cup rolled oats
1 cup Baker's Angel Flake Coconut

Sift flour, baking powder, salt, and soda together. Cream shortening, add sugars gradually, and cream together until light and fluffy. Add egg and vanilla and beat well. Add flour, oats, and coconut and mix thoroughly. Shape dough in small balls and place on ungreased baking sheets. Bake in moderate oven (375°F.) 12 to 15 minutes. Makes 2 dozen cookies.

## Crunchies

*The method of mixing these cookies is unusual — the result is unusually good cookies.*

1½ cups Post Toasties, crushed
¾ cup flour
¾ cup sugar
⅔ cup Baker's Angel Flake Coconut
½ teaspoon salt
½ cup shortening
2 tablespoons light corn syrup
1 teaspoon baking soda
½ teaspoon vanilla

Combine cereal, flour, sugar, coconut, and salt in a bowl. Set aside. Melt shortening in saucepan over medium heat. Add corn syrup; cook and stir until mixture comes to a boil. Then add soda and stir rapidly to blend. When foam settles, remove mixture from heat at once, add vanilla, and blend. Pour over dry ingredients; mix well. (Mixture will be dry and crumbly.)

Press by tablespoonfuls against side of bowl and drop on ungreased baking sheets, placing cookies about 2 inches apart. Press with fork to flatten slightly. Bake in moderate oven (375°F.) 7 to 8 minutes, or until lightly browned. Cool 1 to 2 minutes, then remove cookies with spatula. Makes 2½ dozen.

## Vanilla Nut Icebox Cookies

*Crisp, buttery cookies that can be sliced and baked as you need them.*

2 cups sifted flour
1½ teaspoons Calumet Baking Powder
⅛ teaspoon salt
6 tablespoons shortening
1 cup granulated sugar
¼ cup firmly packed brown sugar
1 egg, well beaten
1 cup chopped nuts
1 tablespoon milk
1½ teaspoons vanilla

Sift flour, baking powder, and salt together. Cream shortening; add sugars gradually, creaming thoroughly. Add egg, nuts, milk, and vanilla; mix well. Add flour gradually, mixing well after each addition. Shape into rolls, 1½ inches in diameter, and wrap in waxed paper. Chill overnight, or until firm enough to slice. Cut in ⅛-inch slices; bake on ungreased baking sheets in hot oven (425°F.) 5 minutes, or until done. Makes about 8 dozen cookies.

***Butterscotch Icebox Cookies.*** Use recipe for Vanilla Nut Icebox Cookies, substituting brown sugar for granulated sugar. Use a total of 1¼ cups firmly packed brown sugar.

*It may be just a friend dropping in for a chat over coffee, or perhaps it's the weekly Kaffeeklatsch — whatever the occasion Pecan Twists (p. 78) are ideal for morning coffee.*

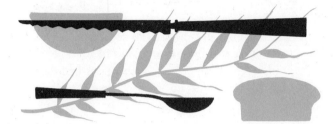

## SECTION 7

GENERAL FOODS
KITCHENS

# The Staff of Life

Of all the spicy, nutty, roasty, toasty aromas drifting from a busy oven, none is quite so mouth-watering as that of homemade breads baking. Because of improved methods and ingredients bread making is no longer the chore it once was, but it remains a source of great pleasure to the baker as well as the family and friends lucky enough to sample the results.

*Yeast:* This is a living organism that leavens breads and makes them light. Now-a-days most of it is packaged in a dry granular form in envelopes. When you buy yeast always check the date on the back of the envelope. Yeast should not be used after this expiration date.

Granular yeast is first dissolved in warm water — water that's comfortably warm to the touch (105° F. to 115° F.). Then when mixed with water, flour, and other ingredients, the yeast begins to ferment and creates carbon dioxide gas. This gas causes the dough to rise, producing light, porous breads. Yeast is also partly responsible for the characteristic aroma

73

and flavor of breads. This fermentation progresses most rapidly at a warm temperature, somewhere between 85°F. and 90°F.

*Flour:* The kind of flour used in bread making is very important. Most yeast doughs are made with all, or at least part, wheat flour because it contains gluten. This is an almost rubbery substance that forms an elastic framework capable of surrounding and holding the carbon dioxide gas bubbles formed by yeast. All-purpose flour should be used for yeast doughs since its gluten content is high. Breads made with rye flour, oats, bran, or cornmeal should always contain some all-purpose flour as a source of gluten. Otherwise the bread will be compact and quite heavy.

*Kneading:* After all the ingredients have been combined most recipes suggest kneading the dough. This is simply mixing and blending by hand a dough that's too stiff to mix with a spoon. Flour your hands and flatten the dough on a lightly-floured surface. Pick up edge of dough farthest from you and fold it toward you. Then press down two or three times with the heels of your hands, pushing the dough away from you. Turn the dough a quarter of the way around, fold it, press, and push again. Repeat this turning, folding, pressing, and pushing motion until the dough becomes satiny smooth and quite elastic. This usually takes about 10 minutes. Keep your hands and the kneading surface lightly floured even though the total amount of flour may be more than the recipe specifies. Flours vary in the amount of liquid they will absorb.

After kneading place the dough in a greased bowl, cover it with a clean towel and put it in a warm place, free from drafts. We place the dough in an unlit oven warmed by a pan of hot water. Now the fermentation starts. When enough gas has been produced to puff the dough up to double its original size, punch the dough down to press out the gas. This breaks up large air pockets so the bread will be fine textured. Now it's ready to shape into rolls or loaves. Let the shaped dough rise again until double in bulk, then bake as directed.

*Batter Bread:* The newest and probably the easiest and quickest yeast breads to make are "batter breads." The ingredients and mixing method are similar to those of standard yeast breads, but the amount of liquid is higher in proportion to the flour. This produces a dough that's relatively soft, soft enough in fact to beat with a spoon or electric mixer. This soft dough requires no kneading because the beating is sufficient to develop the gluten. After the dough has been mixed, beaten, and has risen once stir it down and spread it into a greased casserole, loaf pan, or muffin pans. Let it rise again before baking.

74

## White Bread

*A soft, springy white bread with an excellent flavor and a rich brown crust.*

1 cup milk
2 tablespoons sugar
2 teaspoons salt
2½ tablespoons shortening
1 cup warm (not hot) water
1 package Fleischmann's Active
   Dry Yeast*
6 cups sifted flour (about)

* For faster rising, use 2 packages yeast.

Scald milk. Stir in sugar, salt, and shortening. Cool to lukewarm. Measure warm water into mixing bowl. Sprinkle yeast over water; stir until dissolved. Add lukewarm milk mixture. Stir in 3 cups flour. Beat until smooth. Stir in remaining flour, until dough can be handled easily. Turn out on lightly floured board. Knead until smooth and elastic. Place in greased bowl; brush lightly with melted shortening. Cover with clean towel. Let rise in warm place, free from draft, until doubled in bulk, about 1 hour and 20 minutes.

Punch down and divide into 2 equal portions. Roll or pat out dough, removing air bubbles, to a 9x7-inch rectangle. Then roll firmly, as for a jelly roll, starting on a 7-inch side. Place in greased 8x4x3-inch loaf pan. Cover with a clean towel and let rise in warm place, free from draft, until doubled in bulk, about 55 minutes. Bake in hot oven (400°F.) about 50 minutes. Remove from pans immediately. Brush top crusts with melted margarine or butter. Makes 2 loaves.

*Maple Pecan Rolls (p. 77) are delicious for breakfast, brunch, snacks, and as a special dinner roll when company is expected.*

## White Batter Bread

*A quick, no-knead bread with an interesting open grain and a rough, textured top crust.*

1¼ cups warm (not hot) water
1 package Fleischmann's Active
    Dry Yeast
2 tablespoons soft shortening
2 teaspoons salt
2 tablespoons sugar
3 cups sifted flour

Pour warm water into a large mixing bowl. Sprinkle yeast over water; stir until dissolved. Add shortening, salt, sugar, and 1½ cups flour. Beat 2 minutes at medium speed of an electric mixer or 300 vigorous strokes by hand. Scrape sides and bottom of bowl frequently. Stir in remaining flour and beat with a spoon until smooth, about 1 to 1½ minutes. Scrape batter from sides of bowl. Cover dough with a clean cloth and let rise in a warm place, free from draft, until doubled in bulk, about 30 minutes.

When batter has risen, stir down by beating about 25 strokes. Spread batter evenly in a greased 9x5x3-inch loaf pan. Batter will be sticky. Let rise in warm place, free from draft, until edge of batter reaches ¼ inch from top of pan, about 40 minutes. Bake in moderate oven (375°F.) for 45 to 50 minutes, or until brown. When done, immediately remove from pan. Brush top with melted margarine or butter. Cool. Makes one 9x5-inch loaf.

*Whole Wheat Batter Bread.* Use recipe for White Batter Bread, substituting firmly packed brown sugar for granulated sugar and 1 cup whole wheat flour for 1 cup of the white flour. Add ½ cup of whole wheat flour with the first addition of flour; add the remaining whole wheat flour with the second addition.

*Rye Batter Bread.* Use recipe for White Batter Bread, substituting firmly packed brown sugar for granulated sugar and 1 cup sifted rye flour for ½ cup of the white flour. Add ½ cup rye flour with the first addition of flour; add the remaining rye flour with the second addition. Add 1 teaspoon caraway seeds with first addition of flour, if desired.

*Herb Batter Bread.* Use recipe for White Batter Bread, adding 1 teaspoon caraway seeds, ½ teaspoon nutmeg, and ½ teaspoon powdered sage with the first addition of flour.

## Refrigerator Roll Dough

*A basic roll dough that will keep for a week in the refrigerator. Use it for all sizes and shapes of dinner rolls.*

¾ cup hot water
½ cup sugar
1 tablespoon salt
¼ cup shortening
1 cup warm (not hot) water
2 packages Fleischmann's Active
    Dry Yeast
1 egg, beaten
5¼ cups sifted flour (about)

Combine hot water, sugar, salt, and shortening. Cool to lukewarm. Measure warm water into a large mixing bowl. Sprinkle yeast over water; stir until dissolved. Stir in lukewarm water mixture. Add egg and 2½ cups flour. Beat until smooth. Stir in remaining flour and beat one minute. Dough will be soft. Place dough in greased bowl; brush top with soft shortening. Cover tightly with waxed paper or aluminum foil. Store in refrigerator until doubled in bulk, or until needed. (Dough may be kept 1 week in refrigerator, about 40°F. to 45°F.) To double recipe, double each of the ingredients.

*Pan Rolls.* Divide Refrigerator Roll Dough in half. Form each half into a roll about 16 inches long. Cut each roll into 16 equal pieces. Form into smooth balls. Place ¼ inch apart in 2 greased

8-inch shallow round or square pans. Cover. Let rise in warm place, free from draft, until doubled in bulk, about 1 hour. Brush with melted margarine or butter. Bake in moderate oven (375°F.) about 20 minutes. Makes 32 rolls.

**Fan Tans.** Divide Refrigerator Roll Dough into 3 equal pieces. Roll out each piece into 11x9-inch rectangle. Brush lightly with melted margarine or butter. Cut one rectangle into 7 equal strips, about 1½ inches wide. Pile strips on top of one another. Cut into 6 equal pieces, about 1½ inches long; place cut side up in greased medium muffin pans. Repeat with remaining rectangles of dough. Cover rolls. Let rise in warm place, free from draft, until doubled in bulk, about 1 hour. Brush lightly with melted margarine or butter. Bake in hot oven (400°F.) about 20 minutes. Makes 18 Fan Tans.

**Crescents.** Divide Refrigerator Roll Dough into 3 equal pieces. Roll out each piece into a circle about ¼ inch thick and about 9 inches in diameter. Brush lightly with melted margarine or butter. Cut each circle into 8 wedges. Stretch wide end of wedge slightly; then roll firmly starting at wide end. Seal points firmly. Place 2 inches apart, with point underneath, on greased baking sheets. Curve to form crescents.

Cover. Let rise in warm place, free from draft, until doubled in bulk, about 1 hour. Brush with melted margarine or butter. Bake in hot oven (400°F.) about 15 minutes. Makes 24 Crescents.

**Clover Leaf Rolls.** Divide Refrigerator Roll Dough in half. Form each half into rolls about 12 inches long. Cut each half into 12 equal pieces. Form each of these pieces into 3 small balls and brush with melted margarine or butter. Place 3 balls in each cup of greased muffin pans. Cover. Let rise in warm place, free from draft, until doubled in bulk, about 1 hour. Brush lightly with melted margarine or butter. Bake in hot oven (400°F.) about 15 minutes. Makes 24 rolls.

**Maple Pecan Rolls.** Combine ⅓ cup firmly packed brown sugar, ⅔ cup Log Cabin Syrup, and 3 tablespoons melted margarine or butter; spread in two 8x8x-2-inch pans. Sprinkle ½ cup pecans over mixture in pans. Divide Refrigerator Roll Dough in half. Form each half into a 16-inch roll. Cut each into 16 equal pieces. Form into balls. Place in pans, about ¼ inch apart. Cover. Let rise in warm place, free from draft, until doubled in bulk, about 1 hour. Bake in hot oven (400°F.) about 25 minutes. Turn out of pans immediately. Makes 32 rolls.

*Crusty slices of freshly baked White Bread (p. 75) will disappear like magic. Wonderful for sandwiches and toast.*

## Rich Sweet Dough

*Use this rich dough as the basis for all kinds of sweet rolls and coffee cakes. Several suggestions follow this recipe.*

2 packages Fleischmann's Active
  Dry Yeast
¼ cup warm (not hot) water
1 cup lukewarm milk
1 cup softened margarine or butter
2 eggs, beaten
¼ cup sugar
1 teaspoon salt
1 teaspoon grated lemon rind
4½ cups sifted flour (about)

Dissolve yeast in warm water. Combine dissolved yeast and remaining ingredients in large mixing bowl. Beat until smooth, about 1 minute. Dough will be very soft. Cover with a damp cloth. Place in refrigerator for at least 2 hours, or overnight. Shape as desired.

*Cinnamon Buns.* Divide Rich Sweet Dough in half. Roll each half into a 14x9-inch rectangle. Brush lightly with melted margarine. Combine 1½ cups sugar, 2 teaspoons cinnamon, and ⅔ cup raisins. Sprinkle each oblong with half of the mixture. Roll up from 9-inch side as for a jelly roll. Cut each roll into 9 equal pieces. Place, cut side up, about 1 inch apart in two greased 9-inch layer cake pans or two greased 8-inch square pans. Cover with clean towel and let rise in warm place, free from draft, until double in bulk, about 1 hour. Bake in moderate oven (350°F.) about 35 minutes. Frost with Glossy Confectioners' Sugar Glaze (p. 61). Makes 18 buns.

*Pecan Twists.* Combine ½ cup margarine or butter, ⅔ cup firmly packed brown sugar, and 2 teaspoons corn syrup in saucepan. Bring to a rolling boil. Pour immediately into two 15x10x1-inch jelly roll pans or large oblong pans. Sprinkle with ¾ cup chopped pecans.

Divide Rich Sweet Dough in half.

Roll each half into a 12x12-inch square; brush each with 2 tablespoons melted margarine or butter. Combine ½ cup brown sugar and 2 teaspoons cinnamon; sprinkle center third of each square with 2 tablespoons of the mixture. Fold one-third over the center third of each square. Sprinkle with 2 tablespoons of cinnamon mixture. Fold each remaining third over the two layers. Cut with sharp knife crosswise into strips 1 inch wide. Take hold of each end of strip and twist in opposite directions. Seal ends firmly. Place in prepared pans about 1½ inches apart. Cover. Let rise in warm place, free from draft, until doubled in bulk, about 1 hour. Bake in hot oven (400°F.) about 20 minutes. Invert pan and serve rolls warm. Makes 24 large rolls.

*Date Braided Coffee Cake.* Combine 1 cup chopped pitted dates, ¼ cup firmly packed brown sugar, ⅔ cup water, ½ cup chopped nuts, and 1 tablespoon lemon juice in a saucepan. Bring to a boil over medium heat, stirring constantly. Continue boiling until mixture is thick enough to spread.

Divide Rich Sweet Dough in half. Roll each half into a 16x8-inch rectangle. Spread half the date filling down center third of each rectangle. Cut 15 slits in dough along each side of filling, making strips about 1 inch wide. Fold strips at an angle across filling, alternating from side to side. Place on greased baking sheet. Cover and let rise in warm place, free from draft, until doubled in bulk.

Combine 1 egg yolk and 2 tablespoons milk. Brush cakes with mixture. Combine 2 tablespoons margarine or butter, 2 tablespoons sugar, ⅓ cup sifted flour, and ½ teaspoon cinnamon. Sprinkle half of mixture on each cake. Bake in moderate oven (350°F.) about 35 minutes. Makes 2 cakes.

*Sweet Chocolate Tea Rolls.* Divide Rich Sweet Dough in half. Roll one half into a 10x16-inch rectangle. (Use remaining half of dough for another kind of roll.) Brush lightly with melted margarine or butter and cut into 2-inch squares. Break two ¼-pound packages Baker's German's Sweet Chocolate into squares. Place 1 square of chocolate in the center of each square of dough. Bring 2 opposite corners of dough over the top of the chocolate and pinch to seal tightly. Place on lightly greased baking sheets. Let rise until double in bulk, about 30 minutes. Brush with 1 egg, slightly beaten, and sprinkle with ½ cup slivered almonds.

Bake in hot oven (425°F.) 10 to 12 minutes. Remove from baking sheets and sprinkle with confectioners' sugar. Serve warm. Makes 40 small rolls.

*Whole Wheat Batter Bread (p. 76) is made without kneading. It has a soft, open texture and a delicious nutty flavor.*

*A weekend breakfast or brunch special — a sizzling ham steak and hot buttery Griddlecakes (p. 87) served with lots of syrup.*

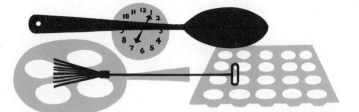

## SECTION 8

GENERAL FOODS
KITCHENS

# Breads in a Hurry

Quick breads are just exactly what their name implies — quick, easy-to-make breads. Unlike regular breads, they do not use yeast but are leavened with either baking powder or baking soda plus an acid. Most quick breads are best when served fresh from the oven, piping hot. They are really not very good cold, although they can be reheated. The most popular quick breads are:

*Biscuits:* These are the most versatile and probably the best known of all the quick breads. They are made from a soft dough consisting of shortening cut into flour sifted with baking powder and salt. Enough liquid, usually milk, is added to make a soft dough that can be handled. The dough is kneaded slightly, then rolled or patted to desired thickness and cut into rounds. Use a floured cutter and use a straight, not a twisting motion, when cutting. Lift the biscuits with a spatula onto an ungreased baking sheet.

Fruit shortcakes, scones, drop biscuits, and various sweet rolls are all variations, more or less, of a basic biscuit recipe.

*Muffins:* The old-fashioned name for this type of bread is "gems." Muffins are made from a stiff batter. The "muffin method" of mixing consists of combining all the dry ingredients (flour, sugar, salt, and baking powder) and adding the combined liquid ingredients (milk, eggs, and *melted* shortening) all at once. The next step, that of mixing, is of utmost importance. Mix *only* until the flour mixture is dampened — the batter usually looks lumpy or pebbly. The more a muffin batter is mixed, the more the gluten is developed. Over-mixed muffins will have a peaked unattractive surface, tunnels, and will tend to be tough.

Another method sometimes used for mixing muffins calls for the fat being cut into the combined dry ingredients. Then the liquid ingredients are added and mixed in quickly.

If muffin batter does not fill all the cups of the pan, we fill the empty ones with water for more even baking. This protects the pans, too.

***Quick bread loaves:*** Most quick breads baked in the shape of a loaf contain nuts and/or fruits. The method of mixing as well as the ingredients and their proportions are similar to muffins. These loaves are the one exception to the quick bread serve-it-hot rule — most of these breads are more moist, slice better, and improve in flavor if they are wrapped, then stored overnight. Don't be alarmed if your fruit or nut bread loaf comes from the oven with a deep crack on top, this is characteristic.

***Pancakes and waffles:*** Although not baked in the true sense, these quick breads do "bake" on a griddle. They are made from soft, necessarily pourable batters. The ingredients are similar to those used in muffins with, of course, a higher liquid level. Just as with muffins, do not overmix pancake or waffle batter. Mix only until ingredients are blended, then quit even if the batter looks lumpy.

Bake pancakes on a hot, not smoking, griddle or skillet. If a drop of water "dances" on the griddle or skillet surface, the temperature is just about right. Electric skillets are ideal for pancakes since the heat is controlled. Most skillets need to be very lightly greased, but only for the first batch of pancakes. Some griddles need no greasing. This is especially true if the batter contains two or more tablespoons of fat.

Using a cup or good-sized ladle, pour each pancake on the griddle in a single motion. (We often mix the batter in a pitcher or a 1-quart measuring cup with a pouring lip to save dish-washing time.) Bake the pancakes until a multitude of tiny bubbles appear on the unbaked side. Turn them only once and bake until browned.

Waffle irons need to be hot before pouring the batter. Most irons come equipped with a temperature indicator. A new waffle iron needs "seasoning"; follow the manufacturer's instructions for this. Greasing a seasoned waffle iron is usually not necessary, but here again follow directions that come with the iron. Never wash waffle iron plates with soap and water, it ruins the seasoning. Use a dry stiff brush instead.

## Baking Powder Biscuits

*As a dinnertime treat serve these light, tender biscuits golden brown and piping hot from the oven.*

2 cups sifted flour
2½ teaspoons Calumet Baking Powder
¾ teaspoon salt
5 tablespoons shortening
¾ cup milk (about)

Sift flour, baking powder, and salt together. Cut in shortening. Add milk and stir with fork until soft dough is formed (about 20 strokes). Turn out on lightly floured board and knead 20 turns. Pat or roll lightly ½ inch thick. Cut with floured 2-inch biscuit cutter. Bake on ungreased baking sheet in hot oven (450°F.) 12 to 15 minutes. Makes 14 biscuits.

*Cheese Biscuits.* Use recipe for Baking Powder Biscuits, adding 1 cup grated American cheese to the dry ingredients with the shortening. Makes 16 to 18.

*Quick-Mix Biscuits.* Measure 2 cups Ever-Ready Blend (see below) into bowl. Add ½ cup milk, then mix, shape, and bake as directed in Baking Powder Biscuits. For Quick-Mix Drop Biscuits, increase milk to ¾ cup. Drop by heaping teaspoonfuls on lightly greased baking sheet. Bake as above. Makes 10 or 12 biscuits.

## Ever-Ready Blend

*This is a basic blend to keep on hand for making all kinds of quick breads, sweet rolls, and coffee cakes.*

2½ tablespoons Calumet Baking Powder
1 tablespoon salt
6 cups (1½ quarts) sifted flour
1 cup shortening

Combine baking powder and salt and mix well. Measure 3 cups of the flour into sifter and add ½ of the baking powder and salt mixture; sift into large bowl. Repeat, sifting remaining dry ingredients together. Cut in shortening with pastry blender or two knives until finely divided and mixture resembles coarse meal. Makes about 7 cups Ever-Ready Blend.

Place in glass jars or crockery bowl and cover lightly with cloth or plate to allow circulation of air. Store in cool, dry place or in refrigerator. Keeps well for 3 or 4 weeks.

*Large Recipe.* Use 12 cups (3 quarts) sifted flour, 5 tablespoons Calumet Baking Powder, 2 tablespoons salt, and 2 cups shortening. Sift flour, 3 cups at a time, with ¼ of baking powder-salt mixture, as above. Makes about 14 cups Ever-Ready Blend.

*For recipes using Ever-Ready Blend see pages 84, 86, 88, 89.*

## Quick Pizza

*A double-quick snack adapted from the Italian original.*

1 cup Ever-Ready Blend
¼ cup milk
1 tablespoon olive or salad oil
3½ cups (1 pound 12 oz. can) whole
    tomatoes, drained
¼ cup grated Parmesan cheese
¾ to 1 cup grated Mozzarella cheese
¼ teaspoon oregano
½ teaspoon salt
¼ teaspoon pepper

Measure Ever-Ready Blend (p. 83) into bowl. Add milk; stir until soft dough is formed. Turn out on lightly floured board and knead 30 seconds. Shape dough into ball and roll into circle about 12 inches in diameter. Place on ungreased baking sheet.

Brush dough with oil. Spread tomatoes evenly over dough. Sprinkle cheeses over tomatoes. Sprinkle with oil. Mix oregano, salt, and pepper and sprinkle over top. Bake in hot oven (425°F.) 15 to 20 minutes. Cut in wedge-shaped pieces. Makes one 12-inch pizza.

## Scones

*Rich, fruit-laced biscuit wedges patterned after the famous Scottish scones.*

1 egg, well beaten
⅓ cup milk
2 cups Ever-Ready Blend
3 tablespoons sugar
1 teaspoon grated lemon or orange rind
½ cup raisins

Combine egg and milk. Measure Ever-Ready Blend (p. 83) into bowl. Add sugar, rind, and raisins. Add milk mixture; stir with fork until soft dough is formed. Turn out on lightly floured board and knead 30 seconds.

Divide dough into two equal parts; pat or roll each into a circle ½ inch thick. With sharp knife, cut each circle into 6 triangles. Place on greased baking sheet. Brush tops with milk or slightly beaten egg white; sprinkle with sugar. Bake in hot oven (450°F.) 10 to 12 minutes. Makes 1 dozen scones.

## Rich Biscuits

*These biscuits are extra rich and flaky — delicious with butter and jam or topped with fruit for shortcake.*

2 cups sifted flour
4 teaspoons Calumet Baking Powder
½ teaspoon salt
½ teaspoon cream of tartar
2 teaspoons sugar
½ cup shortening
⅔ cup milk

Sift flour, baking powder, salt, cream of tartar, and sugar together. Cut in shortening until mixture resembles coarse crumbs. Add milk and stir with fork until soft dough is formed. Turn out on lightiy floured board and pat or roll lightly ½ inch thick. Cut with floured 2-inch biscuit cutter. Bake on ungreased baking sheet in hot oven (450°F.) 10 to 12 minutes, or until golden brown. Makes 16 biscuits.

*Cheese Pinwheels.* Prepare Rich Biscuit dough, adding 1 cup grated Cheddar cheese just before adding milk. Cream together ⅛ teaspoon cayenne, ¼ teaspoon salt, ½ teaspoon paprika, and ¼ cup butter. Divide biscuit dough in half and roll one piece into a 10x14-inch rectangle. Spread with half of butter mixture. Then roll as for jelly roll, starting from 14-inch side. Slice into thin rounds, about ¼ inch thick. Repeat with other half of dough. Bake in hot oven (450°F.) for 10 to 12 minutes. Makes 5 dozen pinwheels.

*Shortcake Biscuits.* Prepare Rich Biscuit dough, increasing sugar to ¼ cup and decreasing milk to ⅓ cup. Beat 1 small egg with milk before adding to flour mixture. Roll and shape as directed. Brush ½ of biscuit rounds with melted butter and top with remaining biscuits. Bake as directed. Separate biscuits. Spoon sweetened fruit between and on top of biscuits. Serve with whipped cream, if desired. Serves 8.

## Peach Biscuit Cobbler

*A baked peach pudding with a rich biscuit top.*

½ recipe Rich Biscuit dough (above)
2 packages (12 ounces each) Birds Eye Sliced Peaches, thawed
1 tablespoon Minute Tapioca
1 tablespoon lemon juice
⅛ teaspoon nutmeg
⅛ teaspoon almond extract
1 tablespoon butter

Turn dough out on lightly floured board and pat or roll lightly to fit top of 1½-quart baking dish. Cut several slits near center of dough.

Combine peaches, tapioca, lemon juice, and nutmeg in saucepan. Cook and stir until mixture comes to a full boil. Add almond extract and pour into greased 1½-quart baking dish. Dot with butter. Adjust dough on hot fruit mixture, opening slits to permit steam to escape. Bake in hot oven (400°F.) for 25 to 30 minutes, or until biscuit topping is done. Makes 6 servings.

## Tea Muffins

*Tiny little muffins with a nutty-wheat flavor — fine tea-time fare.*

1¼ cups sifted flour
2 teaspoons Calumet Baking Powder
½ teaspoon salt
⅓ cup butter or margarine
1 cup firmly packed brown sugar
2 eggs
1 cup Post Grape-Nut Flakes
½ cup milk
1 teaspoon vanilla

Sift flour, baking powder, and salt together. Cream butter thoroughly. Add sugar gradually, creaming well after each addition. Add eggs, one at a time, beating well after each. Mix in cereal. Combine milk and vanilla. Add flour to egg mixture alternately with milk; stir just to moisten all flour.

Spoon batter into muffin pans which have been *well greased* on the bottoms only, filling ⅔ full. Bake in hot oven (400° F.) about 15 minutes. Makes 18.

## Corn Meal Muffins or Corn Sticks

*Take your choice — they're both delicious served hot 'n crispy.*

1 cup sifted flour
¾ cup corn meal
2 teaspoons Calumet Baking Powder
¾ teaspoon salt
2 tablespoons sugar
1 egg, beaten
¾ cup milk
¼ cup melted shortening

Sift flour, corn meal, baking powder, salt, and sugar together. Add egg, milk, and shortening. Stir until blended. (Do not overmix.)
*For muffins,* spoon batter into greased muffin pans, filling ⅔ full. Bake in hot oven (425°F.) 25 minutes, or until lightly browned.
*For corn sticks,* heat greased corn stick pans; pour in batter. Bake in hot oven (450°F.) 20 minutes, or until golden brown. Makes 8 large corn sticks.

*Perfect lunchbox fare — Orange Nut Bread (p. 87) sliced and spread with cream cheese.*

## De Luxe Muffins

*Extra shortening, cut in, not melted, makes these muffins really superb. Try them plain or "fancied."*

2 cups sifted flour
2½ teaspoons Calumet Baking Powder
2 tablespoons sugar
¾ teaspoon salt
½ cup shortening
1 egg, well beaten
¾ cup milk

Sift flour, baking powder, sugar, and salt together. Cut in shortening. Combine egg and milk and add all at once to flour mixture. Then stir *only* until dry ingredients are dampened. Turn into greased muffin pans, filling each about ⅔ full. Bake in hot oven (400°F.) 25 minutes, or until done. Makes 10.

**Blueberry Muffins.** Use recipe for De Luxe Muffins. Fold 1 cup blueberries into batter. Bake as directed. Makes 12.

**Cranberry Muffins.** Use recipe for De Luxe Muffins. Chop 1 cup cranberries, sprinkle with 2 tablespoons sugar, and fold into batter. Bake as directed. Makes 12 muffins.

**Apricot Muffins.** Use recipe for De Luxe Muffins. Add ½ cup cut dried apricots to flour mixture.

**Bacon Muffins.** Use recipe for De Luxe Muffins. Add ½ cup crushed crisp bacon to flour mixture.

**Fruit Muffins.** Use recipe for De Luxe Muffins. Add ⅔ cup finely cut dates or prunes to flour mixture.

**Short-Cut Muffins.** Measure 2 cups Ever-Ready Blend (p. 83) into bowl. Add 2 tablespoons sugar, 1 well-beaten egg, and ¾ cup milk. Mix and fill muffin pans as directed in De Luxe Muffins. Bake in hot oven (425°F.) 20 minutes, or until done. Makes 8 muffins.

## Delicious Nut Bread

*Slices of this quick, nut-studded loaf are wonderful buttered or served sandwich-fashion with cream cheese.*

3 cups sifted flour
3 teaspoons Calumet Baking Powder
1½ teaspoons salt
1 cup firmly packed light brown sugar
1 egg, well beaten
1⅓ cups milk
¼ cup shortening, melted
1 cup finely chopped nuts

Sift flour, baking powder, and salt together. Add brown sugar. Combine egg and milk. Add milk mixture and shortening to flour; then mix enough to dampen flour. Fold in nuts. Turn into 9x5x3-inch pan or into two 8x4x3-inch pans, lined on bottoms with paper. Bake in moderate oven (350°F.) 1 hour and 5 to 10 minutes for large loaf, or about 50 minutes for small loaves. Cool. Wrap in waxed paper and store overnight before slicing.

**Date Nut Bread.** Prepare Delicious Nut Bread, reducing nuts to ½ cup and folding in 1 cup finely cut dates with nuts.

## Chocolate-Fleck Nut Bread

*An elegant bread laced with bits of chocolate and a subtle orange flavor.*

3 cups Ever-Ready Blend
¾ cup sugar
1 egg, beaten
¾ cup milk
½ cup orange juice
1 package (¼ pound) Baker's German's Sweet Chocolate, chopped
¾ cup chopped walnuts
2 teaspoons grated orange rind, optional

Combine Ever-Ready Blend (p. 83) and sugar in large bowl. Combine egg, milk, and orange juice; add to sugar mixture. Beat vigorously about 30 seconds. Stir in chocolate, nuts, and orange rind. Spoon into a well-greased 9x5x3-inch loaf pan. Bake in moderate oven (350°F.) 55 to 60 minutes. Let stand in pan about 15 minutes. Then turn out on rack to cool. Wrap in foil, waxed paper, or saran and allow to mellow a day before slicing.

## Orange Nut Bread

*Orange juice and rind give just the right tartness — raisins and nuts furnish the texture.*

2¼ cups sifted flour
2 teaspoons Calumet Baking Powder
½ teaspoon baking soda
¾ teaspoon salt
¾ cup plus 2 tablespoons sugar
¾ cup chopped nuts
½ cup raisins
¼ cup ground orange rind
1 egg, well beaten
½ cup milk
½ cup orange juice
2 tablespoons shortening, melted

Sift flour, baking powder, soda, salt, and sugar together. Add nuts, raisins, and orange rind. Combine egg, milk, and orange juice. Add to flour mixture with shortening; mix until all flour is dampened and fruit and nuts are well distributed. Turn the batter into greased 9x5x3-inch loaf pan. Bake in moderate oven (350°F.) 1 hour, or until done. Let cool in pan 10 minutes; then turn out of pan and let stand until cold. Wrap in waxed paper or aluminum foil and store overnight before slicing. Makes 1 loaf.

## Delicate Dessert Pancakes

*Here's a dainty dish — thin, miniature pancakes rolled around Maple Butter and topped with bacon or fruit.*

2 eggs, unbeaten
1 teaspoon salt
1 tablespoon sugar
1 cup cold water
½ cup light cream
¾ cup sifted flour

Beat eggs with a beater or electric blender until very light and frothy. Then beat in salt and sugar. Add water and cream alternately with the flour, a small amount at a time, beating well after each addition. Pour batter onto a hot well-buttered griddle, making 3½-inch circles. Bake to a golden brown on each side. Place about 1 tablespoon Maple Butter on rough side of each pancake and roll up. Serve as a dessert with fruit, or for breakfast with crisp bacon strips, if desired. Makes 4 luncheon servings, 5 pancakes each, or 6 dessert portions, 3 pancakes each.

*Note:* Batter may be stored in refrigerator. Beat thoroughly before using.

**Maple Butter.** Beat ½ cup softened butter or margarine and a dash of salt with a wooden spoon until smooth. Add 1 cup Log Cabin Syrup gradually, about 1 tablespoon at a time, beating well after each addition. Total beating time should be about 10 minutes. Serve with pancakes. Makes 1½ cups.

## Griddlecakes

*A stack of fluffy light griddlecakes, lots of butter, and a pitcher of syrup — now there's a breakfast sensation.*

1¼ cups sifted flour
1½ teaspoons Calumet Baking Powder
¾ teaspoon salt
1 tablespoon sugar
1 egg, well beaten
1 cup milk
3 tablespoons melted shortening

Sift flour, baking powder, salt, and sugar together. Combine egg and milk; add to flour along with shortening. Mix just until flour is dampened. (Batter will be lumpy.) Bake on hot greased griddle until brown on both sides. Turn only once. Serve with butter and Log Cabin Syrup. Makes 10 to 12. *Note:* For thinner griddlecakes, increase milk as desired.

**Jiffy Pancakes.** Measure 2 cups Ever-Ready Blend (see p. 83) into a bowl. Combine 2 well-beaten eggs and 1¼ cups milk; add to Ever-Ready Blend. Mix and bake as directed in Griddle-cakes recipe. Makes about 8 pancakes.

**Cheese Griddlecakes.** Prepare Griddle-cakes as directed, adding ½ cup grated sharp Cheddar cheese to batter.

**Waffles.** Prepare Griddlecakes as directed, baking in a hot waffle baker. Makes 4 large waffles.

**Bran Griddlecakes.** Prepare Griddle-cakes as directed, reducing flour to 1 cup and adding ¾ cup Post 40% Bran Flakes to the sifted dry ingredients. Makes 8 to 10 griddlecakes.

**Buttermilk Pancakes.** Prepare Grid-dlecakes as directed, reducing flour to 1 cup. Sift ⅛ teaspoon baking soda and ⅛ teaspoon cream of tartar with the dry ingredients and substitute butter-milk for whole milk.

**Blueberry Pancakes.** Prepare Griddle-cakes as directed. Increase sugar to 2 tablespoons. Fold ⅔ cup thawed drained frozen blueberries into batter.

*Rich De Luxe Muffins (p. 86) studded with bits of dried fruits will lend interest to breakfast, dinner, and tea menus.*

## Honey Bran Kuchen

*Serve this hot from the oven as a special treat for Sunday breakfast.*

¾ cup sifted flour
2½ teaspoons Calumet Baking Powder
¼ teaspoon salt
½ cup milk
¼ cup honey
1 egg, well beaten
3 tablespoons melted shortening
2 cups Post 40% Bran Flakes
¼ cup firmly packed brown sugar
½ teaspoon cinnamon
¼ to ½ teaspoon nutmeg
2 tablespoons melted butter or margarine

Sift flour, baking powder, and salt together. Combine milk, honey, and egg. Add to flour mixture along with short-ening. Mix *only* enough to dampen flour. Fold in 1½ cups of the cereal. Pour into greased 8x8x2-inch pan.

Mix together brown sugar, spices, butter, and remaining ½ cup cereal. Sprinkle over top of batter and bake in hot oven (400°F.) 25 minutes, or until done. Makes 8 servings.

## Coconut Filbert Coffee Ring

*A rich biscuit dough shaped into a ring and filled with a sweet coconutty filling. A weekend breakfast special.*

2 cups sifted flour
2½ teaspoons Calumet Baking Powder
1 teaspoon salt
⅓ cup granulated sugar
⅓ cup shortening
1 egg, slightly beaten
⅓ cup milk
3 tablespoons butter or margarine, melted
¼ cup firmly packed brown sugar
¼ cup chopped filberts
¾ cup Baker's Angel Flake Coconut

Sift flour, baking powder, salt, and granulated sugar together. Cut in the shortening. Combine egg and milk. Add to flour mixture and stir until soft dough is formed.

Turn out on lightly floured board and knead 30 seconds. Roll out in an 18x9-inch rectangle. Brush with 2 tablespoons melted butter. Spread with a mixture of brown sugar, nuts, and ½ cup coconut. Roll as for jelly roll, wetting edges to seal. Bring the ends together to form ring and place on ungreased baking sheet. Cutting from outside in with scissors, cut 1-inch slices almost through the ring. Turn each slice cut side down. Brush with remaining 1 tablespoon melted butter.

Bake in hot oven (400°F.) for 20 to 25 minutes. Remove to cake rack. Spread with Glossy Confectioners' Sugar Glaze (p. 61) while ring is still hot. Toast remaining ¼ cup coconut; sprinkle over glaze. Makes 8 servings.

## Butterscotch Pecan Rolls

*Biscuits pinwheeled with cinnamon-sugar and glazed with a pecan topping.*

3 cups Ever-Ready Blend
¾ cup milk (about)
2 tablespoons butter or margarine
⅓ cup firmly packed brown sugar
¼ cup butter or margarine
¼ cup firmly packed brown sugar
½ cup chopped pecans

Measure Ever-Ready Blend (p. 83) into bowl. Add milk; mix until soft dough is formed. Turn out on lightly floured board; knead 30 seconds. Roll into rectangle ¼ inch thick. Cream 2 tablespoons butter and ⅓ cup brown sugar together; spread on dough. Roll as for jelly roll; cut in 1-inch slices.

Meanwhile, melt remaining ¼ cup butter in 8x8x2-inch pan. Add remaining ¼ cup brown sugar and mix well. Sprinkle nuts on top. Place rolls in pan, cut side down. Bake in moderate oven (375°F.) 35 minutes, or until done. Invert at once onto plate. Let stand 1 minute; remove pan. Makes 12 rolls.

## Fruit-Filled Coffee Cake

*A rich biscuit dough laced over a tart-sweet filling, then glazed. Serve hot!*

⅓ cup chopped, cooked prunes
⅔ cup finely chopped apples
⅓ cup firmly packed brown sugar
⅓ cup water
2 teaspoons lemon juice or vinegar
⅛ teaspoon salt
⅛ teaspoon cinnamon
3 cups Ever-Ready Blend
½ cup granulated sugar
1 egg, slightly beaten
½ cup milk

Combine prunes, apples, brown sugar, water, lemon juice, salt, and cinnamon; cook 5 minutes, stirring frequently. Remove from heat. Cool.

Combine Ever-Ready Blend (p. 83) and granulated sugar in bowl. Combine egg and milk and add to sugar mixture; stir until soft dough is formed. (If necessary, add a little more milk.) Place on lightly floured board and knead 30 seconds. Place on lightly floured baking sheet and roll into 15x10-inch rectangle.

Spread filling down center of rectangle. Cut 15 one-inch slits in dough along each side of filling. Fold strips at an angle over filling, alternating strips from side to side. Bake in moderate oven (375°F.) 40 minutes, or until done. While hot, brush lightly with ½ recipe Glossy Confectioners' Glaze (p. 61), if desired. Makes 8 to 12 servings.

*Tart, tangy lemon filling, made from scratch or from a mix, in tender flaky pastry and topped off with a golden brown meringue make dessert something really to look forward to.*

SECTION 9

GENERAL FOODS
KITCHENS

# Pretty Pastries

Pies, as we know them, are distinctively an American dessert. True, Europeans have their tarts, *Chaussons,* and flans which are similar, but they are not pies.

The most important single factor in a pie is the pastry — the flour, shortening, and water variety. Pie crusts made with graham crackers and the like are delicious but present no challenge. The woman who makes tender, flaky, golden brown pie crust deserves and gets respect in any culinary circle. There is no secret to making a perfect pastry, unless the secret is following directions exactly. Here are a few suggestions that will help you turn out pastry of which you can be proud.

*Mixing:* When you bite into pastry that has all the characteristics of leather, chances are that one of two things has happened. First, the gluten in the flour has been overdeveloped. This usually happens if the fat has not been thoroughly *cut* into the flour. We find a pastry blender most efficient, but two knives can be used with equal success. Use a cutting motion as if you were cutting through the flour — at this stage particles of the mixture should be clumped together in pieces about the size of small peas.

A high proportion of water will also make pastry tough. Sprinkle the water on the flour mixture about a teaspoon at a time while tossing the mixture with a fork. Never "stir" in the water. Add only enough water so that the mixture can be formed into a ball. Overmixing and handling pastry create tough pastry, too, so treat it gingerly.

*Rolling:* A pastry cloth to cover the board and a stockinet-covered rolling pin make pastry easier to roll, but they are not necessary. Any surface and a rolling pin lightly dusted with flour will do. Roll out only enough pastry for a single crust at a time. Roll pastry from the center to the edges, rolling until quite thin — less than ⅛ inch thick. The circle should be large enough to extend 1½ inches all around the edge of an inverted pie pan. The pastry may be transferred to the pan either by rolling it around the rolling pin or by folding it into quarters.

*Fitting:* Fit the pastry in the pan loosely, stretching will cause shrinkage during the baking. For single crust pies trim so that about 1 inch extends over the edge of the pan. Fold the extra pastry under, press together to form a high standing rim, then flute. (See page 93 for fancy edges.) Trim the bottom crust of a two-crust pie even with the pie pan rim. Center the top crust over the filling, then trim the edges so that ½ inch of pastry extends over the rim.

To seal the edges of a double crust pie, moisten the bottom edge and press top and bottom edges together, then fold the edge of the top crust under the bottom crust and press together firmly. Flute. Allow the steam that forms when baking a double crust pie to escape by cutting slits in the top crust. If you have an artistic bent, make a pretty pattern of the slits.

*Baking:* Single crust pie shells need to be pricked with a fork before baking to prevent buckling. Do not prick bottom crust of a double crust pie. When we want a shiny, attractive glaze on a pie, we brush the top crust with egg white, beaten with a little water or cream. If the fluted edge of the crust browns too quickly, cover it with aluminum foil for the remaining baking time.

Despite precautions juicy fruit pies frequently boil over. A sheet of aluminum foil strategically placed on the rack below to catch drips saves a lot of post-baking clean-up time.

After the pie crust is all made, there are usually scraps of pastry left over — these are a wonderful source of snack and nibble foods. Press the scraps of pastry together and roll smooth. Then cut in strips and sprinkle with grated cheese. Bake on an ungreased baking sheet in a hot oven (450°F.) about 12 minutes, or until browned.

# Frilly Edgings

*Fluted:* Form a high standing rim on a single or double crust pie. Place right index finger on inside of rim, left index finger and thumb on outside. Press pastry with right index finger into a V formed by pinching dough with left thumb and index finger. Repeat all around rim.

*Scalloped:* Form a high standing rim on a single or double crust pie. Place left index finger and thumb on inside of rim ¾ to 1 inch apart. Pull pastry between left thumb and finger toward center of pie with right index finger, forming a scallop. Repeat all around rim.

*Coin:* Trim overhanging pastry on a single crust pie even with the pan edge. From trimmings, cut dime-size circles and overlap around slightly moistened edge of pastry. Press lightly with finger tips.

*Rope:* Form a high standing rim on a single or double crust pie. Then press right thumb into rim at an angle and at the same time press pastry against thumb with knuckle of right index finger.

*Patterned:* Form a high standing rim on either a single or double crust pie. Press tines of a fork into pastry rim at about ½- to ¾-inch intervals all around rim.

93

## Flaky Pastry

*Tender flaky pastry is a thing of beauty and a joy forever. Measure carefully and follow instructions.*

2¼ cups sifted flour
1 teaspoon salt
¾ cup shortening
7 tablespoons cold water

Combine flour and salt. Cut in about ½ cup of the shortening, using a pastry blender or 2 knives, until mixture resembles coarse meal. Add remaining shortening in several pieces and cut in until mixture is the size of large peas.

Sprinkle with water, a small amount at a time. Mix lightly with a fork until all particles are moistened and cling together when pastry is pressed into a ball. Amount of water may vary with flours. Cover with damp cloth, and let stand a few minutes.

Roll out pastry very thin (less than ⅛ inch thick) on lightly floured surface. Makes enough pastry for one 9-inch two-crust pie, two 9-inch pie shells, or fifteen 3½-inch tart shells.

*For two-crust pie,* roll out half the pastry very thin. Press into a 9-inch pie pan and trim pastry at edge of rim. Roll out remaining pastry very thin and cut several 2-inch slits or a fancy design near center. Fill pie shell. Moisten edge of bottom crust. To adjust top crust, fold pastry in half or roll loosely on rolling pin; center on filling. Open slits with a knife. (Well-opened slits are important to permit escape of steam during baking.) Trim top crust, allowing it to extend ½ inch over rim. To seal, press top and bottom crusts together on rim. Then fold edge of top crust under bottom crust and flute. Bake in hot oven (425°F.) 50 to 60 minutes, or as recipe directs.

*For pie shell,* prepare half recipe of Flaky Pastry. Roll out pastry very thin. Press into a 9-inch pie pan, trim pastry 1 inch larger than pan, fold edge to form a standing rim, and flute. Prick pastry with fork, pricking all over and very thoroughly around the bottom curve of pan. Bake in hot oven (450°F.) for 12 to 15 minutes, or until lightly browned. Cool before filling.

*For tart shells,* roll out pastry very thin. Cut 5- to 6-inch rounds of pastry and fit carefully on outside of tart or muffin pans. Trim edges. Prick with fork. Place on baking sheet and bake in hot oven (450°F.) for 12 to 15 minutes, or until lightly browned.

*For a two-crust 8-inch pie,* use the Flaky Pastry recipe, decreasing ingredients to 2 cups flour, ¾ teaspoon salt, ⅔ cup shortening, and 6 tablespoons cold water. Prepare and bake as directed for a two-crust 9-inch pie.

## Graham Cracker Crumb Crust

*The easiest of all pie crusts to make — perfect for no-bake cream fillings.*

1¼ cups fine graham cracker crumbs
2 tablespoons sugar
⅓ cup butter or margarine

Combine crumbs and sugar. Add butter and mix well. Press firmly with back of spoon on bottom and sides of 9-inch pie pan. Bake in moderate oven (375°F.) 5 to 8 minutes. Cool before filling.

*Note:* For an 8-inch crust, use 1 cup crumbs, 2 tablespoons sugar, and ¼ cup melted butter or margarine.

**Unbaked Graham Cracker Crust.** Make crumb mixture as directed for Graham Cracker Crumb Crust. Press firmly on bottom and sides of pan or shallow freezing tray. Chill crust for 1 hour before filling.

**Gingersnap Crumb Crust.** Use recipe for Graham Cracker Crumb Crust. For a 9-inch pie crust, use 1¼ cups fine gingersnap cooky crumbs, 3 tablespoons sugar, and ¼ cup melted butter or margarine. For an 8-inch pie crust, use 1 cup crumbs, 2½ tablespoons sugar, and 3 tablespoons melted butter.

***Vanilla Wafer Crumb Crust.*** Use recipe for Graham Cracker Crumb Crust. For a 9-inch pie crust, use 1¼ cups fine vanilla wafer crumbs, 1 tablespoon sugar, and ¼ cup softened butter or margarine. For an 8-inch pie crust, use 1 cup crumbs, 1 tablespoon sugar, and 3 tablespoons softened butter.

***Chocolate Crumb Crust.*** Use recipe for Graham Cracker Crumb Crust. For a 9-inch crust, use 1¼ cups chocolate cooky crumbs, 2 tablespoons sugar, and ¼ cup melted butter.

## Coconut Meringue Shell

*A crisp, chewy meringue shell — an impressive setting for cream fillings and for fruit.*

⅔ cup Baker's Angel Flake Coconut
¼ cup sifted confectioners' sugar (about)
2 egg whites
¼ teaspoon cream of tartar
Dash of salt
⅔ cup granulated sugar
½ teaspoon vanilla

Roll coconut in enough confectioners' sugar to coat lightly; set aside. Combine egg whites, cream of tartar, and salt in bowl. Beat until foamy throughout. Add granulated sugar, 2 tablespoons at a time, beating well after each addition. Then continue beating until mixture stands in very stiff peaks. Fold in vanilla and the sugar-coated coconut. Spread mixture on bottom and sides of a lightly greased 9-inch pie pan. Bake in slow oven (325°F.) about 30 minutes, or until shell feels dry and firm. Cool. To serve, fill with ice cream, fruit, or cream filling. Garnish with additional coconut, if desired.

***Coconut Meringue Shells.*** Prepare Coconut Meringue Shell. Shape the meringue mixture into six 3-inch rounds on unglazed paper on baking sheet. Make a deep depression in center of each and build up sides about 1½ inches high. Bake as directed.

## Quick Coconut Crust

*An easy-to-make crust — crisp and delicious. Bake it or not as you see fit.*

¼ cup butter or margarine, melted
2 cups Baker's Angel Flake Coconut

Combine butter and coconut. Press evenly into an 8- or 9-inch pie pan. Bake in slow oven (300°F.) for 30 to 35 minutes, or until golden brown. Cool.

To serve, fill crust with chiffon or cream pie filling; chill until firm. Or just before serving, fill with ice cream, using 1½ pints for an 8-inch crust and 1 quart for a 9-inch crust.

## Cherry Crisscross Pie

*A rosy-red cherry pie with a peek-a-boo top made of pastry strips.*

4 teaspoons Minute Tapioca
1 cup sugar
⅛ teaspoon salt
3 cups (2 cans, 16 oz. each) drained
    water-packed pitted sour cherries
½ cup cherry juice
6 drops red food coloring
¼ teaspoon almond extract, optional
Pastry for two-crust 9-inch pie
1 tablespoon butter or margarine

Combine tapioca, sugar, salt, cherries, cherry juice, food coloring, and almond extract. Mix thoroughly and let stand about 15 minutes.

Roll out half of the pastry very thin (less than ⅛-inch thick). Line a 9-inch pie pan and trim pastry about ½-inch larger than rim. Roll out remaining pastry very thin. Cut into ½-inch strips. Fill pie shell with cherry mixture. Dot with butter.

Moisten edge of bottom crust. Arrange pastry strips in lattice across top of pie. Fold edge of bottom crust over ends of strips, press together, and flute. Bake in hot oven (425°F.) 50 minutes, or until crust is golden brown and pie filling bubbles near center. Serves 6 to 8.

## Amber Apple Pie

*Apples and spice in a no-bake, delightfully different apple pie.*

1 package (3 ounces) Apple
   Jell-O Gelatin
1 to 2 tablespoons sugar
¼ teaspoon salt
⅛ teaspoon cinnamon
⅛ teaspoon nutmeg
1 cup boiling water
8 to 12 large ice cubes
½ teaspoon lemon juice
2 cups diced fresh apples (about 3)
1 baked 9-inch pie shell

Combine Jell-O, sugar, salt, cinnamon, and nutmeg. Add boiling water; stir until Jell-O is completely dissolved. Add ice cubes and stir constantly 2 to 3 minutes, or until Jell-O starts to thicken. Remove unmelted ice. Add lemon juice and let stand 2 to 3 minutes. Then add apples. Stir. Pour into pie shell. Chill until set, about 3 hours. Garnish with prepared Dream Whip or whipped cream, if desired. Serves 6 to 8.

*Ice cream and instant pudding mix supply the delicate strawberry flavor in this luscious Ice Cream Pie (p. 101).*

## Coconut Dutch Apple Pie

*An old-fashioned, open-face apple pie with a spicy, baked-on coconut topping.*

2 tablespoons flour
½ cup sugar
⅛ teaspoon salt
1 teaspoon cinnamon
5 cups tart apple slices, ¼ inch thick
1 unbaked 9-inch pie shell
1 tablespoon lemon juice
1 tablespoon butter or margarine
¼ cup sugar
½ cup sifted flour
¼ cup butter or margarine, melted
¾ cup Baker's Angel Flake Coconut

Combine 2 tablespoons flour, ½ cup sugar, the salt, and cinnamon. Place a layer of apples in pie shell and sprinkle with part of flour-sugar mixture. Layer remaining apples alternately with flour-sugar mixture. Sprinkle lemon juice over pie and dot with 1 tablespoon butter. Bake in hot oven (425°F.) 45 minutes, or until apples are tender.

Combine ¼ cup sugar and ½ cup flour. Add melted butter and mix until crumbly. Add coconut. Sprinkle over baked pie. Return to oven and bake 8 to 12 minutes longer, or until browned. Makes 6 to 8 servings.

## Coconut Custard Pie

*There's nothing better than a good Coconut Custard Pie. This one is superb!*

4 eggs, slightly beaten
⅓ to ½ cup sugar
¼ teaspoon salt
3 cups milk
1 teaspoon vanilla
1⅓ cups (about) Baker's Angel
   Flake Coconut
1 unbaked 9-inch pie shell

Combine eggs, sugar, salt, milk, vanilla, and coconut. Mix well. Pour into pie shell. Bake in hot oven (425°F.) 30 minutes, or until custard is set. Cool. Makes 6 to 8 servings.

## Blueberry Pie

*Frozen blueberries have made this pie, once a seasonal New England favorite, a popular year 'round dessert.*

¼ cup Minute Tapioca
¼ cup granulated sugar
2 tablespoons firmly packed
  brown sugar
¼ teaspoon salt
⅛ teaspoon cinnamon
Dash of cloves, optional
½ cup blueberry juice
2 packages (12 oz. each) frozen
  sweetened blueberries, thawed and
  drained — about 2½ cups
1 tablespoon lemon juice
Pastry for 2-crust 8- or 9-inch pie
1 tablespoon butter or margarine

Combine tapioca, sugars, salt, spices, blueberry juice, blueberries, and lemon juice. Let stand about 15 minutes. Roll out half of pastry very thin (less than ⅛ inch thick). Line an 8- or 9-inch pie pan. Trim pastry at edge of rim. Roll out remaining pastry very thin. Cut several 2-inch slits or a fancy design near center. Fill pie shell with fruit mixture. Dot with butter. Moisten edge of bottom crust. Center top crust on filling. Open slits with a knife. (Well-opened slits are important to permit escape of steam during baking.) Trim top crust, letting it extend ½ inch over rim. To seal, press top and bottom crusts together on rim. Then fold edge of top crust under bottom crust and flute. Bake in hot oven (425°F.) about 50 to 60 minutes, or until top is well browned. Serves 6 to 8.

## Fruit Pies

*Fresh rhubarb, peach, grape, or berry pie.* Combine 3½ cups prepared fruit, 1½ to 2 tablespoons Minute Tapioca, 1 to 1¼ cups sugar, ¼ teaspoon salt, and 1 tablespoon melted butter. Let stand 15 minutes, or while pastry is being made. Use as filling for 9-inch two-crust pie.

*Canned peach, plum, or pineapple pie.* Combine 2½ cups canned fruit (drained), 1 cup fruit juice, 2½ tablespoons Minute Tapioca, sugar to sweeten, ⅛ teaspoon salt, and 1 tablespoon melted butter. Let stand 15 minutes, or while pastry is being made. Use as filling for 9-inch two-crust pie.

## Lemon Cheese Pie

*The tang of lemon gives this creamy cheese pie a just-right flavor lift. A wonderful hurry-up party dessert.*

1 large package (8 oz.) cream cheese
2 cups milk
1 package Jell-O Lemon Instant Pudding
1 baked 8- or 9-inch Graham
  Cracker Crust

Place cream cheese in a bowl and stir with a fork until well softened. Add ½ cup of the milk, a little at a time, blending until mixture is very smooth. Then add remaining 1½ cups milk and the pudding mix. Beat with egg beater just until well mixed, about 1 minute. Pour into crust. Chill until set. Makes 6 to 8 servings.
*Lemon Cream Cheese Pie.* Prepare Lemon Cheese Pie as directed. Use 1 pint of sour cream in place of the milk.

## Chocolate Angel Pie

*A rich, milk chocolate filling framed in a crisp, chewy meringue makes an impressive, festive dessert.*

1 package (¼ pound) Baker's German's
  Sweet Chocolate
3 tablespoons water
2 egg yolks, beaten
1 cup whipping cream
1 tablespoon confectioners' sugar
⅛ teaspoon cinnamon
9-inch Coconut Meringue Shell

Place chocolate and water in saucepan over low heat. Stir until chocolate is melted. Remove from heat. Gradually stir egg yolks into the chocolate mixture. Continue cooking over low heat for one minute, stirring constantly. Cool.

Combine whipping cream, sugar, and cinnamon in chilled bowl. Beat until cream is stiff but still glossy. (Do not overbeat.) Spread about 1 cup of cream in the bottom of meringue shell. Fold remaining cream into the chocolate mixture and spread over cream in shell. Chill several hours or overnight. Garnish with additional whipped cream, if desired. Makes 6 to 8 servings.

## Chocolate Party Meringue Pie

*Attention chocolate lovers! Here's a pie to please you — deep rich chocolate filling topped with a fluffy meringue.*

1 package Jell-O Chocolate Pudding and Pie Filling
2 tablespoons firmly packed brown sugar
½ square Baker's Unsweetened Chocolate
2 cups milk
2 egg yolks
2 tablespoons butter or margarine
1 baked 8-inch pie shell
2 egg whites
4 tablespoons granulated sugar

Combine pie filling mix, brown sugar, chocolate, and ¼ cup of the milk in saucepan. Add egg yolks and blend well. Then add remaining 1¾ cups milk. Cook and stir over medium heat until mixture comes to a *full* boil. Remove from heat. Blend in butter. Cool about 5 minutes, stirring once or twice. Pour into pie shell.

Beat egg whites until foamy throughout. Add granulated sugar gradually, 2 tablespoons at a time, beating well after each addition. Then continue beating until meringue stands in stiff peaks. Pile on filling and spread to edge of pie crust. Bake in hot oven (425°F.) 5 to 10 minutes, or until delicately browned. Serves 6.

## Miracle Peach Pie

*Peaches and cream in tender, flaky pastry — mmmm-m-m-m good.*

1 package (12 oz.) Birds Eye Sliced Peaches, slightly thawed
1¼ cups water
1 package Jell-O Vanilla Pudding and Pie Filling
¼ teaspoon salt
2 teaspoons lemon juice
1 tablespoon butter or margarine
¼ teaspoon almond extract
1 baked 8-inch pie shell

Cut slightly thawed peaches into bite-size pieces. Add to ½ cup of the water in a saucepan. Bring to a boil. Meanwhile, combine pudding mix, salt, lemon juice, and remaining ¾ cup water. Stir to form a smooth paste. Add to boiling fruit, stirring to blend. Then cook and stir until mixture comes to a *full* boil.

Remove from heat and add butter and almond extract. Cool 5 minutes. Pour into pie shell. Let stand about 3 hours, or until firm. Garnish with prepared Dream Whip or sweetened whipped cream, if desired. Serves 6.

## Lemon Meringue Pie

*The perfect dessert for any occasion — tart-sweet lemon pie topped off with toasted meringue.*

⅓ cup cornstarch*
1¼ cups sugar
Dash of salt
1½ cups hot water
3 egg yolks, slightly beaten
1 tablespoon butter or margarine
2 teaspoons grated lemon rind
⅓ to ½ cup lemon juice
1 baked 9-inch pie shell
3 egg whites
6 tablespoons sugar

* Or use ½ cup sifted flour

Combine cornstarch, 1¼ cups sugar, and the salt in a medium saucepan.

*Jiffy Cream Tarts (p. 103) made with pudding and pie filling mix get a touch of glamour with shaved sweet chocolate.*

Gradually stir in hot water. Bring to a boil over high heat. Then reduce heat and cook until thick and clear — about 10 minutes. Remove from heat. Stir several spoonfuls of the hot mixture into the egg yolks and mix well. Pour back into saucepan. Bring to a boil. Then reduce heat and cook 4 to 5 minutes, stirring constantly. Remove from heat. Stir in butter and lemon rind. Gradually add lemon juice. Cool 5 minutes; then pour into pie shell.

Beat egg whites until foamy throughout. Add 6 tablespoons sugar, 2 tablespoons at a time, beating after each addition until blended. Continue beating until mixture stands in stiff peaks. Pile on filling and spread to edge of pie crust. Bake in a hot oven (425°F.) 5 to 10 minutes, or until delicately browned. Cool thoroughly — at least 4 hours. Makes 6 to 8 servings.

## Lemon Chiffon Pie

*Frozen lemonade concentrate furnishes the tangy lemon flavor in this refreshingly light dessert.*

1 tablespoon (1 envelope) gelatin
¼ cup cold water
½ cup sugar
2 egg yolks
1¼ cups milk
½ cup thawed Birds Eye Concentrated Lemonade
½ cup whipping cream
2 egg whites
¼ teaspoon salt
4 tablespoons sugar
1 baked 9-inch pie shell

Soften gelatin in cold water. Combine ½ cup sugar and the egg yolks in saucepan. Add milk gradually, stirring constantly. Cook and stir over medium heat until mixture coats spoon. (Do *not* boil.) Pour over gelatin and stir until gelatin is dissolved. Then add concentrated lemonade. Chill until slightly thickened. Whip cream until stiff but still glossy and fold into chilled mixture.

Beat egg whites with salt until foamy throughout. Add 4 tablespoons sugar, 2 tablespoons at a time; beat well after each addition. Then continue beating until stiff peaks form. Fold into lemonade mixture. Turn into pie shell. Chill until firm. Serve garnished with sweetened whipped cream or prepared Dream Whip, if desired. Serves 6 to 8.

## Mocha Chiffon Pie

*Coffee and chocolate are perfect flavor mates teamed in this delicate pie.*

1 tablespoon (1 envelope) gelatin
¼ cup cold water
1 tablespoon Instant Maxwell House Coffee
1 cup (6-oz. package) Baker's Semi-Sweet Chocolate Chips
1 cup milk
¼ teaspoon salt
2 egg yolks, beaten
2 egg whites
¼ cup sugar
½ cup whipping cream
1 baked 9-inch pastry shell

Soften gelatin in cold water. Combine instant coffee, chocolate chips, milk, and salt in a saucepan. Place over *low* heat and stir constantly until chips are melted. Add small amount of hot mixture to egg yolks, stirring vigorously. Then gradually add remaining mixture, stirring constantly. Return mixture to saucepan and cook and stir over low heat until slightly thickened — about 5 minutes. Remove from heat, add softened gelatin, and stir until dissolved. Chill until slightly thickened.

Beat egg whites until foamy; add sugar gradually and continue beating until stiff peaks form. Whip the cream until stiff but still glossy. Fold egg whites and cream into chilled mixture. Pour into pie shell. Chill until firm. Serve garnished with additional whipped cream, if desired. Serves 6 to 8.

## Pecan Pudding Pie

*Thick with chopped pecans, this pie is a variation of the Southern delicacy that's become a national favorite.*

1 cup dark corn syrup
1 package Jell-O Vanilla Instant Pudding
¾ cup evaporated milk
1 egg, slightly beaten
1 cup chopped pecans
1 unbaked 9-inch pie shell

Blend syrup with pudding mix in bowl. Gradually add evaporated milk and egg, stirring to blend. Add pecans and pour into pie shell. Bake in moderate oven (375°F.) until pie is set, about 55 minutes. Serves 6 to 8.

## Chocolate Bavarian Pie

*A two-toned, fluffy-textured pie with a mild, milk chocolate flavor.*

1 tablespoon (1 envelope) gelatin
⅔ cup sugar
¼ teaspoon salt
1¾ cups milk
1 package (¼ pound) Baker's German's Sweet Chocolate
3 egg yolks, slightly beaten
3 egg whites
1 teaspoon vanilla
⅔ cup Baker's Angel Flake Coconut
1 baked 9-inch pie shell

Combine gelatin, ⅓ cup of the sugar, the salt, and milk in top of a double boiler. Add chocolate. Cook over hot water until chocolate is melted and gelatin is completely dissolved. Blend well with egg beater. Gradually add to egg yolks, stirring constantly. Return mixture to double boiler and cook 3 minutes longer, stirring constantly. Cool about 10 minutes.

Beat egg whites until foamy. Add remaining ⅓ cup sugar gradually and continue beating until mixture stands in stiff peaks. Fold in chocolate mixture gradually, blending well. Add vanilla and coconut. Spoon into pie shell. Chill about 2½ hours or until firm. Top with Cocoa Whipped Cream (p. 60) and additional coconut, if desired. Serves 6 to 8.

## Strawberry Ice Cream Pie

*A party-fare pie with a delicate strawberry flavor.*

1 cup milk
1 pint strawberry ice cream
1 package Jell-O Vanilla Instant Pudding
1 baked 9-inch pie shell or graham cracker crumb crust

Combine milk and ice cream in bowl. Blend until smooth. Add pudding mix and beat slowly with egg beater just until well mixed, about 1 minute. Pour immediately into pie crust. Chill until set — about 1 hour. Garnish with strawberries, if desired. Serves 6 or 8.

## Raisin Turnovers

*Raisins and spices with just a hint of orange flavor make these old-fashioned turnovers taste as good as they look.*

1¾ cups seedless raisins
1¾ cups water
¼ cup orange juice
⅓ cup firmly packed brown sugar
1 tablespoon Minute Tapioca
½ teaspoon cinnamon
¼ teaspoon salt
1 tablespoon vinegar
1 tablespoon butter or margarine
2 teaspoons grated orange rind
Pastry for two-crust 9-inch pie

Combine raisins, water, and orange juice in saucepan. Bring to a boil and boil 5 minutes. Then add sugar, tapioca, cinnamon, and salt. Cook and stir until mixture again comes to a boil. Remove from heat. Add vinegar, butter, and orange rind; blend. Cool.

Roll out pastry very thin (less than ⅛ inch thick) and cut into 6-inch circles or 5-inch squares. Moisten edges with cold water. Place about 3 tablespoons filling on one side of each circle or square, fold over, and seal edges with floured fork. Brush lightly with cream, if desired. With sharp knife, make slits in top of each turnover to permit escape of steam. Bake in hot oven (425°F.) about 20 minutes. Serve with prepared Dream Whip, whipped cream, or ice cream, if desired. Makes 8 to 10 turnovers.

## Cream Puffs and Eclairs

*Mocha Cream Puffs.* Prepare 1 package Swans Down Vanilla Cream Puff-Eclair Mix according to the package directions, adding 2 tablespoons Instant Maxwell House Coffee to the filling mix before cooking.

*Chocolate Eclairs.* Prepare 1 package Swans Down Vanilla Cream Puff-Eclair Mix according to the package directions, adding 2 squares Baker's Unsweetened Chocolate and 2 tablespoons sugar to the filling mix before cooking.

*Lemon Coconut Cream Puffs.* Prepare 1 package Swans Down Lemon Cream Puff-Eclair Mix according to the package directions, adding ⅔ cup Baker's Angel Flake Coconut to the filling mix before cooking. Sprinkle ⅓ cup coconut over topping, if desired.

*Pineapple Eclairs.* Prepare 1 package Swans Down Lemon Cream Puff-Eclair Mix according to the package directions, substituting ¼ cup pineapple juice for the water. Fold 1 can (8½ oz.) drained crushed pineapple into the cooked filling before chilling.

*Make Blueberry Pie (p. 97) a year 'round treat with frozen blueberries. A fancy design cut in the top crust allows steam to escape during baking.*

## Petit Jam Tarts

*A delicious snack-time sweet — fragile pastry folded over a jam filling.*

½ pound butter or margarine
1 package (8 oz.) cream cheese
Pinch of salt
2 cups sifted flour
Jam (about one 10-oz. jar) — apricot, raspberry, or strawberry
Milk

Cream butter, cream cheese, and salt together. Add flour gradually, mixing until smooth. Form dough into a ball and wrap in waxed paper. Chill at least 3 hours. Divide dough in half. Roll out very thin and cut with a 2½-inch round cooky cutter or cut into 3-inch squares. Place a small amount of jam in the center of each circle or square. Brush edges of dough with a little milk. Fold half of dough over and seal edges together with tines of fork. Place on ungreased cooky sheets and bake in a moderate oven (375°F.) for about 15 minutes, or until lightly browned. Cool. Makes about 5 dozen tarts.

102

## Strawberry Tarts

*Strawberries served in little tart shells with an unusual whipped topping.*

1 egg white
¼ cup sugar
½ cup whipping cream
½ teaspoon vanilla
1⅓ cups (about) Baker's Angel
  Flake Coconut
1 package (10 oz.) Birds Eye Sliced
  Strawberries, thawed
5 baked 3½-inch tart shells

Beat egg white until foamy throughout. Add sugar, 2 tablespoons at a time, beating well after each addition. Then continue beating until stiff peaks form. Whip cream; add vanilla, and fold into meringue mixture. Add 1 cup of coconut. Place strawberries in shells; top with cream mixture and remaining coconut. Serve at once. Makes 5 tarts.

## Jiffy Cream Tarts

*Speedy little tarts with a tempting creamy filling. Choose a flavor to suit yourself and the occasion.*

1 package Jell-O Vanilla (Butterscotch,
  Chocolate, Chocolate Mint, or Coconut
  Cream) Pudding and Pie Filling
1¾ cups milk
¼ cup whipping cream
6 or 7 baked 3½-inch tart shells

Combine pie filling mix and milk in saucepan. Cook and stir over medium heat until mixture comes to a *full* boil. Remove from heat. Pour into bowl. (To avoid surface film, place waxed paper directly on surface of hot pudding.) Chill. Beat slowly with rotary egg beater. Then whip cream and fold into pudding. Spoon into tart shells. Garnish with additional whipped cream, if desired. Makes 6 or 7 tarts.

*Ready for eating now — or 2 months from now. Paisley
Chocolate Cake (p. 25) filled with Peppermint Topping (p. 61)
stays fresh for months if properly wrapped and frozen.*

**SECTION 10**

# Bake Now-Eat Later

In the past few years the biggest boon to the baking homemaker has been the home freezer. The old-fashioned bake day that was a weekly or semi-weekly event in almost all homes has been revived, but in a modified manner. The lucky woman whose kitchen is equipped with a freezer can make three pies instead of just one, a batch of rolls in addition to the loaf of bread, and some cupcakes along with a cake. All of these extras can go into the freezer for some feast of the future.

Almost all baked products freeze well. Some are better if frozen before they are baked, others better if frozen after they are baked. Freezing retains the fresh quality of baked products to a remarkable degree if properly handled. However, it does *not* improve the flavor and texture of baked products. Therefore, freeze products the day they are baked.

***Packaging:*** One of the most important factors in freezing is the packaging — the kind of material used, the wrapping, and the sealing. The wrapping material must be moisture- and vapor-proof, strong and tough, odorless, tasteless, and easy to handle. Some of the most popular materials are: polyethylene plastic bags, plastic- or wax-coated heavy paper, heavy duty aluminum foil, and plastic film. There are, in addition, plastic, glass, and aluminum containers that can be used for semi-liquid substances such as the dough for drop cookies or a pumpkin pie filling.

**A.**

**B.**

We have found the "drug store wrap" the easiest and the best way to wrap for freezing. Place the rolls, cake, or cookies in the center of the paper. Bring the two longest sides together and fold these edges over about ½ inch. Continue folding over as many times as necessary to bring the paper tight and flat against the product. Fold corners toward one another, then fold ends under and stretch tight.

Seal edges of the package with freezer or masking tape and label the package with the date and the product. To seal plastic bags, first press out as much air as possible, then twist the top tightly and secure with a rubber band, soft string, or commercial closers specifically designed for this purpose.

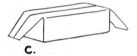

**C.**

**D.**

*Breads:* Both yeast and quick breads can be frozen. Generally the length of storage should not exceed 3 months. Freeze breads after they are baked or partially baked. Unbaked dough can be frozen, but it is risky since both yeast and baking powder may lose all or part of their leavening power during long freezing. We often partially bake yeast rolls — up to the point where they start to brown, then freeze them. These are similar to commercial brown-and-serve rolls. When ready to serve, we simply place them, while frozen, in the oven and bake until they are browned.

*To freeze:* Remove baked product from pan(s) to cool thoroughly. Then pack in family-size amounts and freeze immediately. The longer it stands after it is baked, the less fresh it will taste when served.

*To thaw:* Thaw breads at room temperature while still wrapped. It will take from 1 to 3 hours depending upon the warmth of the room and the size of the product. Frequently loaves can be sliced while still frozen, thus enabling you to thaw only what is needed for one meal. Sliced bread thaws almost immediately. Rolls, muffins, biscuits, and coffee cakes can be thawed in the wrapper at room temperature, or they can be thawed unwrapped in the oven. Place unthawed on a baking sheet and heat at 350°F. for about 15 to 30 minutes, according to the size of the product.

**Cakes:** All kinds and shapes of cakes freeze well. They may be frozen frosted or unfrosted, although with frosted cakes certain precautions must be taken. Avoid freezing cakes frosted with Seven Minute or other boiled frostings; when frozen, they tend to break down and become sticky. Butter cream and fudge frostings, on the other hand, are ideal for freezing. Unfrosted cakes will remain in top condition for at least 3 months. Since aging improves fruit cakes, they will keep indefinitely when frozen. Frosted cakes stored for more than 1 to 2 months are apt to lose quality. Custard-filled cakes are not ideal for freezing since these fillings have a tendency to break down and make the cakes soggy.

*To freeze:* Cool all cakes thoroughly before wrapping. Wrap cake layers separately or wrap them together with a double thickness of saran or waxed paper between each layer. Place cakes in cardboard boxes for additional protection. Freeze frosted cakes (whole or cut) *unwrapped* until the frosting has set, then wrap and seal. Storing frosted cakes in a cardboard box is even more imperative since frozen frosting has a tendency to chip or crack if bumped.

When freezing frosted cakes, we often cut them in halves or quarters. This way, a small portion of a cake can be defrosted and eaten while the rest stays frozen and fresh. Protect the cut cake edges by covering them with saran or waxed paper.

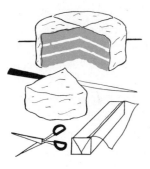

*To thaw:* Frosted cakes should be thawed unwrapped simply because the frosting is apt to stick to the paper when thawing. Thaw unfrosted cakes wrapped since moisture will collect on the surface and make the crust soggy. Unfrosted layers, cupcakes, and loaves thaw in about ½ to 1 hour at room temperature, while frosted layer cakes take up to 3 hours to thaw. Frosted cakes that have been cut in quarters before freezing thaw rapidly. Frozen cakes cut easily with a serrated knife and the pieces thaw in mere minutes.

*Wrap and seal cakes in freezing paper, then place them in la-beled boxes for protection while frozen. These Angel Food loaves are wonderful for all kinds of impromptu desserts.*

**Cookies:** Cookies freeze exceedingly well either baked or unbaked. Freezing baked cookies seems a waste of precious freezer space since few, if any, cooky jars suffer from being overstuffed for any length of time. If a recipe makes a large batch of cookies, bake a third or half the batch, then freeze the rest unbaked. Properly wrapped cookies and cooky dough will keep perfectly for 6 months to a year.

*To freeze:* Baked cookies may be frozen in sheet wrappings, plastic bags, or in containers. Some paper padding avoids broken cookies. Be sure cookies are completely cool before packing. Thaw cookies, while still wrapped, about 15 minutes. Crisp cookies may be heated on a baking sheet for about 5 minutes at 375°F.

Unbaked cookies may be frozen before or after they are shaped. Shape or drop cookies and place them on sheets. Freeze them until frozen solid (1 to 2 hours). Then remove from sheet, wrap, seal, and return the unbaked cookies to the freezer. Bar cooky dough may be frozen right in the pan. Bar, drop, and shaped cookies may all be baked without thawing; simply follow directions, adding a minute or two to the baking time.

Refrigerator cooky dough can be shaped into rolls, wrapped, then frozen. Slice off as many cookies as you want (rolls may need to be thawed slightly) and bake. Return unbaked portion to freezer for another day.

Cooky dough may be frozen in containers, plastic bags, or sheet wrappings. When ready to use, thaw dough to room temperature or temperature required for easiest handling and proceed according to directions.

*Pies:* All manner of fruit, mince, chiffon, and pumpkin pies freeze well. Cream pies can be frozen with some success, but we don't recommend it. Do not freeze custard pies. The filling separates, making the crust quite soggy and the appearance unattractive.

*To freeze pie crusts:* Pastry may be frozen in bulk, rolled out in circles, or fitted and fluted in a pie pan. Stack pastry circles with 2 pieces of saran or waxed paper between each layer so one pastry circle may be removed without thawing the whole batch. Place the stack on a piece of cardboard, wrap, and seal. To use a pastry circle thaw completely at room temperature, then fit into pie pan and proceed as recipe directs.

Pastry in a pie pan, either baked or unbaked, should be frozen solid while unwrapped to avoid damage during wrapping. Avoid trying up all of your pie pans by either using disposable aluminum foil pans for freezing, or by taking the frozen shell out of the pan before wrapping. Frozen pie shells may be stacked before wrapping if crumpled paper is placed between each shell. In freezing pastry in this manner, there is always danger of breakage. We minimize breakage by stacking the shells in a cardboard box.

Neither baked nor unbaked pie shells need thawing. Place unbaked pie shells in the oven (oven-proof glass pie pans should first stand 5 to 10 minutes at room temperature) and bake as recipe directs, adding about 5 minutes to the baking time. Prick shell with a fork after 5 minutes baking. Thaw baked shells at room temperature or heat about 10 minutes in oven.

*To freeze pies:* Prepare crust and filling for fruit and chiffon pies as recipe directs, using a regular pie pan or an aluminum foil pan specifically made for freezing. Do not slit top crust of fruit pies before freezing. Allow the filling of chiffon or similar type pies to set completely before freezing. Be sure baked pies are completely cool before freezing. Meringue toppings for pies do not freeze well, so we freeze only the filling and crust. Then, just before serving, we top the pie with a meringue and brown it in a hot oven.

 To protect the tops of baked or unbaked pies, we cover them with either a paper plate or aluminum pie pan, then wrap and seal. Keep pies level until frozen solid. If the pie is very fragile, freeze unwrapped until solid, then wrap and seal.

*To thaw pies:* Thaw chiffon or other pies with unbaked fillings unwrapped in the refrigerator 1 to 1½ hours. Chiffon pies are sometimes eaten while still partially frozen.

Unwrap baked fruit pies and heat them in a 375°F. oven for about 30 minutes, or until center is hot. Unwrap unbaked fruit pies and place, while still frozen, in a hot oven (425°F.). Bake 40 to 60 minutes according to the type and size of pie. Slit tops of double crust pies before baking.

# Index

111

112

115

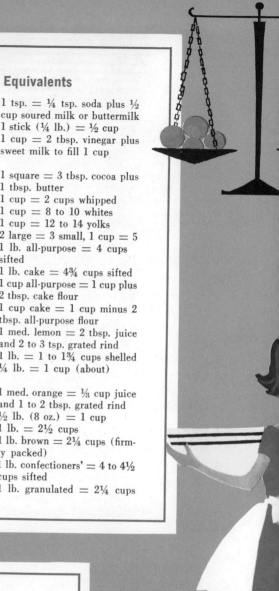

## Handy Equivalents

| | |
|---|---|
| Baking Powder | 1 tsp. = ¼ tsp. soda plus ½ cup soured milk or buttermilk |
| Butter or margarine | 1 stick (¼ lb.) = ½ cup |
| Buttermilk | 1 cup = 2 tbsp. vinegar plus sweet milk to fill 1 cup |
| Chocolate (unsweetened) | 1 square = 3 tbsp. cocoa plus 1 tbsp. butter |
| Cream, heavy | 1 cup = 2 cups whipped |
| Egg whites | 1 cup = 8 to 10 whites |
| Egg yolks | 1 cup = 12 to 14 yolks |
| Eggs, whole | 2 large = 3 small, 1 cup = 5 |
| Flour | 1 lb. all-purpose = 4 cups sifted |
| | 1 lb. cake = 4¾ cups sifted |
| | 1 cup all-purpose = 1 cup plus 2 tbsp. cake flour |
| | 1 cup cake = 1 cup minus 2 tbsp. all-purpose flour |
| Lemon juice and rind | 1 med. lemon = 2 tbsp. juice and 2 to 3 tsp. grated rind |
| Nuts in shell | 1 lb. = 1 to 1¾ cups shelled |
| Nut meats | ¼ lb. = 1 cup (about) |
| Orange juice and rind | 1 med. orange = ⅓ cup juice and 1 to 2 tbsp. grated rind |
| Salad oil | ½ lb. (8 oz.) = 1 cup |
| Shortening | 1 lb. = 2½ cups |
| Sugar | 1 lb. brown = 2¼ cups (firmly packed) |
| | 1 lb. confectioners' = 4 to 4½ cups sifted |
| | 1 lb. granulated = 2¼ cups |

## Oven Temperature Chart

| | |
|---|---|
| Slow | 300°F. - 325°F. |
| Moderate | 350°F. - 375°F. |
| Hot | 400°F. - 425°F. |
| Very Hot | 450°F. - 500°F. |